DREAM BIGGER

BE A REBEL ON PURPOSE

LINDA BREEDLOVE

DREAM BIGGER - BE A REBEL ON PURPOSE

First printing

LIBRARY AND ARCHIVES CANADA
CATALOGUING IN PUBLICATION

ISBN: 978-1-989540-13-8

Credits:
Lance Sullivan - *Concept Photo*: Author and Cover Photos
Adrienne Guinn - *Vital Image Photography*: Glamour Photos
Sierra Bready - Scenic Photos

Published and printed in Canada by
BestSellers Publishing Academy
Publisher: Lucia Monica Gorea, PhD
E-mail: monica.artistic@gmail.com
Author E-mail: Lindabreedlove50@gmail.com

To order a copy of
DREAM BIGGER – *BE A REBEL ON PURPOSE*
please contact the author, Lindabreedlove50@gmail.com,
or the publisher.

Formating and Layout by **Nonon Tech & Design**

TABLE OF CONTENTS

DREAM BIGGER - BE A REBEL ON PURPOSE

The Journey Continues

It's never too late to begin again. It's never too late to find your purpose. It's never too late to reinvent yourself. If it brings you joy, GO FOR IT! You might as well do whatever the hell you want to do, and be happy with your life!

A flower begins as a seed; the plant grows and blooms, then spreads its seeds for more flowers. We must be like that flower—grow, bloom, and spread our seeds; grow some more.

My first book, *Embrace the Journey, Be a Rebel on Purpose* began as a way for me to find more happiness and contentment. Along the path of writing this book, I discovered that, to be really happy and content with my life, I had to find my purpose.

It was not until I was almost finished writing my book that I realized I had found my purpose and passion: writing. I discovered that I had this creative energy surging within me; that I had found what I was searching for. My purpose was to write, yes, but also to be a motivational voice for other people who were seeking their purpose. I realized that I had suppressed my passion for many years. I just needed to find that spark, ignite that passion, and find my purpose.

The spark was the feedback I received on social media posts I'd made to help in my self-discovery. I found that I was helping other women and men ignite their spark as well. That spark began a roaring fire within me that could not be extinguished.

It did not just hit me one day though—it was a gradual process.

Day by day, I began to understand how much I loved to write. It was not easy to put my words and feelings on paper. I always thought that I was a very private person, but now I can share my thoughts, dreams, and experiences without feeling like I have compromised my internal desire for privacy.

I am also conquering my fear of rejection. I am conquering my worry about what other people will think of me. I stopped worrying about being judged for my actions. I realized that, if I was constantly troubled by what other people thought of me, my life was not mine. I now base my happiness on my own accomplishments—NOT other people's opinions. Most people begin thinking that they are at the end of their life at this age, but my life is just beginning.

> "The greatest prison people live in,
> is the fear of what others think."
>
> — UNKNOWN

I have learned to say goodbye to the people who do not bring a positive vibe into my life. I have learned to commit to my dreams and goals, and never look back. I have discovered that, no matter what we do, people will always talk about you, so you might as well give them something to talk about.

I discovered many other things as well. I discovered that to be really happy and content, you must have a passion. With passion, you find your purpose. I learned that while you might have the ability to do something that you desire, you will not do it unless you have the motivation. I also learned that with motivation you must have discipline, because motivation will take you only so far. Discipline propels you to the finish line.

I do not like to say, "searching for yourself." I prefer to say, "looking for your purpose." Most of us do not have a clue what our purpose is. Most of us believe our purpose is to just live day by day and do what is expected of us—expected to get married, have babies, and raise a family. We are expected to be the super-mom and super-wife that society expects. Today, we are expected to have a career as well as a family. We are required to handle all of it with grace, class, and without complaint.

I do realize that there are many women whose greatest desire is to be a wife and a mother, and I admire them for that. I admire that they can do exactly what it is that they want to do. I also admire the women who can balance their home life with their careers and be happy with what they are doing. I tried to do all that, and I always came up short on the contentment part. It wasn't that I was miserable all the time—you make your own happiness, because happiness really does come from within, not from outside sources. I knew how to make myself appear happy. I could always put on a brave face. I just knew that I needed something more in my life.

Growing up, I had a domineering father who expected perfection from his children—especially me, since I was the eldest of my four siblings. I was expected to do all the things that my mother usually did. She worked most days from 2pm to 9pm. I learned to cook dinners when I was 12 years old. I learned to keep the house spotless, and the laundry and ironing done. I learned to take good care of my younger brothers and sister. I had to not only make my own lunch for school the next day, but my father's and siblings', as well. I would finally be able to do my homework when everyone else was tucked into bed, and my father was snoring in front of the television set. There were times when I'd be too tired to do my homework, and as a result, the next day I would get my backside whipped or my knuckles smacked with the yardstick by my teacher.

I dreamed about being free. I dreamed about traveling. I dreamed about life without responsibilities. I did know that my father loved me, but I longed for the day that I would be only responsible for myself. I lived in my dream world of desiring change, but it took me a long time to figure out how to affect the changes I desired. When I finally figured it out, I was married with two small boys, and I knew that yet again, I had other responsibilities, and change was in the distant future once more. So, I kept dreaming.

Now it's time to turn all those dreams into goals and put action behind them in order to get what I want.

My first book talks about my desire for change, and how I managed to accomplish the changes I desired. In this book, I will talk more about the positive changes I am making in my life, and how I am keeping the changes that I want to keep, while discarding the unwanted ones. Yes, that is correct. You may have made some changes in your life, but it doesn't mean you have to keep all of those changes. We humans are constantly evolving, and if we do not make changes continually with ourselves to go along with that, we will be left behind.

If a change that you made in the past is not serving you as you desire it to, then change it again. You have the right to do that. You owe your past nothing.

Remember, you owe your past nothing.

"It's your road, and yours alone,
others may walk it with you,
but no one can walk it for you."

— RUMI

CHAPTER 1

"If you're looking for inspiration, look to your surroundings; look at what you already have. It's all there right in front of you."

— LINDA BREEDLOVE

When I am mentally tired and I need inspiration, I love to go to the ocean. Thankfully, the ocean is only a few minutes away from where I live—I can be there every day that I wish to be.

The following is what I wrote in my journal to help myself on days where I had difficulty finding inspiration to write:

"Inspiration comes in waves, like the ocean. Sometimes those waves come crashing into the shore, and I excite myself with all the ideas I get from watching them cover the shoreline with their fury. Other times the water gently laps closer and closer to me, and slowly I begin to formulate my next plan of action for my book. My head fills with ideas and quotes that I cannot wait to share with everyone."

Sometimes to find the inspiration I seek, I go for a walk, and simply discover and enjoy what nature has to offer me.

Other times you just need to step out into your backyard. Simply enjoy the beauty that surrounds you every day. Be thankful for what you have. Put things into perspective. Listen carefully to your heart. Sometimes motivation happens when you take a precious moment and listen carefully to the silence.

Sometimes you need to change your surroundings for a little while. Meet new people. Pay attention and listen intently to what others have to say. Interact with people who inspire and motivate you. Ask them what inspires them.

Eliminate distractions. Distractions will only add to your inability to be inspired. Find a quiet place in your surroundings, away from all others. Put on some soothing music, or listen to Rock and Roll—whatever makes you happy.

Learn how to meditate. Practice affirmations that help your positive mindset. Spend time reading that book that you have been wanting to read. Take the pressure off yourself to get inspired. Just let it happen. Stop thinking that you must do it all in one day. You have plenty of time. Do not force yourself. The inspiration will come to you just at the perfect time—when it is meant to.

If you cannot find the motivation to do it today, then find something else to do. Keep yourself busy, and do not think about your lack of inspiration. It will happen.

There is always tomorrow. As my mother used to say, **"Tomorrow is another day. You will have another chance to make it right. Life will go on."**

She also said, "Take each day as it comes, and don't sweat the small stuff." That is something that I work on all the time.

"The reason most people never
reach their goals is that they don't define them,
or seriously consider them as believable
or achievable. Winners can tell you
where they are going, what they plan to do
along the way, and who will be sharing the
adventure with them."

— DENNIS WAITLEY

CHAPTER 2

> "Life isn't about finding yourself.
> Life is about creating yourself."
>
> — GEORGE BERNARD SHAW

I am learning that the only way to keep finding my purpose is to constantly be rediscovering things about myself. It is possible to reinvent yourself all the time. I found that I needed to self-evaluate regularly. Self-evaluation is necessary for growth. Look deep within yourself to find out what you need to know to make the changes you desire for yourself. I regularly re-evaluate myself to make sure that the changes I have made are ones I wish to keep.

Do not lose yourself in the chaos of everyday life. Do not settle for the mundane. Do not just wish your life away. Turn those wishes into actual goals. Determine what goals you really want, and work hard to attain them. Dig deep within yourself to discover your own potential.

You must ask yourself: Is where you're going right now where you want to go? Do you want to continue along the same path that you have been following, or do you want to acquire a new route? Do you wish to climb the mountain, or do you wish to stay at the bottom and look at the summit, wishing you were there? Do you want to be able to look back on your life and say that you made the right choices, or do you want to look back and wish that you had made different ones?

The most important step to self-discovery is to take care of yourself. Do not let yourself get lost in the pandemonium of everyday life and forget that you are important. **You are just as important** as everyone else around you. As a matter of fact, it is far more important to take care of yourself first; then, you can be there for others.

Taking care of yourself is as simple as allowing yourself some downtime from doing all the things that are required of you as a person, spouse and parent.

Prioritize yourself. Make yourself the most important person for a day. Spend the entire day on yourself, doing whatever you want. Do whatever makes you happy, not what makes everyone else happy. Make your heart happy. Spoil yourself just for that one day, and do not concern yourself with anyone else. They will get along simply fine without you. You are not being selfish. Do not think that for one moment. You are only taking care of yourself, so you can take care of everything else and everyone else that needs your attention later on.

Never, ever feel guilty for taking care of yourself first, and doing what is best for you.

"Twenty years from now you will be more disappointed by the things that you didn't do than by the things you did do, so throw off the bowlines, sail away from safe harbor, catch the trade winds in your sails. Explore, Dream Discover."

— MARK TWAIN

CHAPTER 3

"When things change inside you,
things change around you."

— UNKNOWN

Transforming yourself is never an easy task. However, it is an ongoing process. You must be open to change constantly.

Change can be a frightening process. We all get comfortable where we are. We might not be satisfied with our present situation, but we are afraid to change it for fear of failing, or fear of the unknown.

What if I fail in my endeavours? What if I do not make it to where I want to be? Will I be considered a failure? What if I will be making a huge mistake?

If you truly desire to change your present situation, you can simply toss those fears aside, and begin by taking little steps toward a better you. You will be a better you, because you will be empowered and happy with yourself for taking charge of your life.

Take each day as it arrives. It does not matter if you go slowly; it only matters that you keep going.

Yes, you will have setbacks. I had many times that I thought slipping back into the "old me" would just be easier. Less hassle.

You will have many times when you feel nothing is going in your favor. You will sometimes feel like you would be better off staying in your present situation because you feel comfortable there. Making changes can be extremely difficult and uncomfortable.

Life has a way of just happening around us. We all have the choice to stop and let life just pass us by, or we can choose to take charge and keep going forward. It all depends on how badly we want the change. Life will always have many twists and turns. You will always have setbacks, but if you keep focused on your desired outcome, what you truly desire will happen. I know, because I have been there, too.

Do not let anyone or anything stop you from achieving your goals. Your own mind and your own thoughts can even be your enemy. Do not listen to your mind when it is telling you that you cannot do what you want to do. Keep those goals in your utmost thoughts, and never let yourself become passive about them. Keep your energy high, and remember that you are a force to be reckoned with. You are a rebel on purpose.

The struggles that you have will be worth it in the end. If you do have setbacks, just remember that every new day is a brand-new beginning. You can start all over again every day. You can reach your goals if you just keep going ahead.

I knew I had to make changes in my life, and I was not sure how to do it. I simply began with taking each day as it came. I repeated my goals to myself every morning and kept a positive mindset that I would accomplish what I had set out to do. I know that changing myself is a journey. Change does not happen overnight. Change does not happen all at once. It is a process.

We are all works in progress, but change will keep happening for me because I know deep in my heart that I am worth it, and I truly desire it.

Writing my first book was way out of my comfort zone. It took a lot of self-talk to allow myself to be made vulnerable by writing my journey to happiness and contentment. I had to step out of my comfort zone and write from my heart. I had to get personal. I had to allow myself to be vulnerable and lay myself open to scrutiny. I had to open my heart.

I found that, by taking small steps every day, I was able to make my dream of writing a book a reality.

It did not matter how long it took me to complete it. It only mattered that I did.

CHAPTER 4

"Your purpose in life is to find your purpose and give your whole heart and soul to it."

— BUDDHA

We all want to have a purpose in life. We all want to feel like what we do is important. We all want to know that we matter.

The first thing you should know about yourself is that you are you. You are not me; you are not your neighbor. You are not your mother, or your father. Everything that you do is entirely up to you, and no one else can be you, or do it for you. You must be yourself. You will spend the rest of your life with yourself, so you must learn to love yourself first.

Do not lose yourself in the chaos of living your everyday life. The world moves rapidly now. Everything is fast-paced. Do not get lost in the whirlwind. Remember who you were before your life became complicated with careers, relationships, children, and everything else that comes with responsibility. Remember the child that you once were.

You do not want to merely survive. You want to thrive. I am talking about going after your own dreams, goals, and desires. To do this, you must take care of yourself first. Then go and find your passion. Be brave enough to begin again, if you are not happy with your present situation. You deserve to have everything that you desire in life. You deserve to have respect. You deserve to be noticed for who you are, not for being someone's parent or spouse. You deserve to have your own identity.

I had to learn that I am important. I had to learn to love myself again. It wasn't that I disliked myself; I just needed to understand in my heart that what I was doing with my life was significant. I did matter. I had to stop comparing myself with other people. I had to stop letting others control me.

Find out what makes you happy. Find out what makes you feel your best. Find out what makes your life exciting. Trust in your heart more. Your heart knows who you are, and what you truly desire. Embrace the uncertainty. Shock yourself and others around you.

Do what brings you joy. Live your best life. Remember who you are. Remember who you were before life got complicated. Find that healthy balance and enjoy your life to the fullest.

Be the person who you want to be. Be the best that you can be. Do not settle for anything less.

> "We cannot become what we want by remaining what we are."
>
> — MAX DEPREE

I keep this quote as my phone's wallpaper, so I can read it many times a day. It's my daily reminder that, if I want to change something in my life, I can do it if I truly desire it enough.

If you have been thinking about doing something or changing something in your life, and you seem to have it in your thoughts constantly, then you need to do it!

Let go of the negative thoughts that keep telling you that you cannot do it. Let go of the negative people that tell you that you should not do it. Let go of the negative naysayers that say it cannot be done. Tell yourself that you can do anything that you want to do, if you really have a desire to do it.

You may have to venture out of your comfort zone to accomplish what you want to do. Do it if the desire will not leave your thoughts. Do not give up on yourself. You might be struggling with the idea, but if you cannot get it out of your mind, if it occupies your thoughts constantly, **then you must do it!**

When I discovered that I had a burning desire to write, I simply began. I kept going until I had written an entire book.

I amazed myself that I accomplished that goal.

I came way out of my comfort zone, and I did it!

All too often we underestimate ourselves and think of all the reasons why we're incapable of doing something. Each one of us has it in us to do what we really want to do, if we desire it enough.

Stop just thinking about what you want to do. Stop talking yourself out of doing what it is that you really have a burning desire to do. Get a firm grip on your desires and goals and go make them happen.

Life is too short to just let all your dreams and goals slide by without at least trying to accomplish them. You do not want to look back on your life and say, "I really wish I had done that."

Do not live with regret. Regretting something that you really wanted to do will haunt you in your later years.

One of the biggest regrets of people on their deathbeds is that they wished they had the courage to live their lives the way they wanted, not the way others wanted them to live it.

CHAPTER 5

> "To me, beauty is about being comfortable in your own skin. It's about knowing who you are and accepting who you are."
>
> — ELLEN DEGENERES

I am prompted to write about this after hearing about a beautiful young girl who thought she had to lose weight because someone told her that she was getting too fat. She ended up with bulimia. She was only twelve years old.

That brought back a memory of a time my mother had a friend over for coffee. I was about twelve or thirteen years old, contentedly drawing pictures and keeping an eye on my younger siblings while my mother and her guest chatted. The friend made a comment that shattered me. She leaned over to my mother and said that she should keep an eye on me, because I was getting too fat. I do not remember what my mother said to her, but I do remember her friend's comment very well.

I kept this comment in my subconscious for years, well into my adulthood. That comment always bothered me. It would resurface time and time again when I found myself in the center of attention, or having to do something I had not done before. I often felt that I was not good enough, slim enough, or beautiful enough. I was active enough as a teenager, but I was always just a little overweight by about ten or fifteen pounds.

As an adult, I put on more weight after having two babies and I did not bother to lose it immediately after. I thought that perhaps I was just destined to be overweight for the rest of my life. "It is in my genes," I said to myself. I always blamed my heredity. Consequently, I became overweight for most of my adult years. I tried to lose weight several times, but it always came right back on, and more when I ended the diet. I finally found the correct way to lose weight and keep it off forever when I was well into my mature years. I learned that I had to make major changes in my lifestyle. I discovered that most diets do not work because diets are temporary. I learned that you must change your lifestyle if you want lasting changes. Changing your lifestyle is permanent if you work at it. Even so, I still had to learn to be comfortable in my own skin.

Today, I feel beautiful, I feel slim, and I feel confident. Please though, I am not advocating everyone must lose weight! You do not have to lose weight to feel beautiful. However, if you truly desire to do it, keep focused on the outcome, and take it all day by day.

I did not learn how to do all that until extremely late in my life.

One thing I do know for sure is that we must empower our children to be strong against negative comments that could destroy their confidence and self-esteem. Tell them that the negative comments are about the other person's lack of confidence; not a reflection of themselves. Tell your children that what other people think of them is based on that person's own personal experiences; not theirs.

If my journey can help someone else become more confident with themselves, then I have succeeded. Lessons that I learned throughout my journey are that you do not have to lose weight to feel beautiful. You do need to have a kind heart and a beautiful soul. If you feel confident on the inside, you will be beautiful, and look confident on the outside.

Beauty and confidence truly do come from within.

"Your self-worth is determined by you. You don't have to depend on someone else telling you who you are."

— BEYONCE

CHAPTER 6

"Autopilot is great for flying planes.
Not so great for living life. Start living your
authentic life and live purposely."

— ELLE SOMMER

For years I lived on autopilot, doing the same things every day. Get up, feed the children, take them to school, and go to work. Come home, make dinner, take the children to their respective sports practices. Go home, get everyone ready for bed, do the laundry, make the lunches for the next day, and go to bed. Then wake up and do it all over again. Every. Single. Day.

I felt like I was not in control of my own life. Someone else was driving my vehicle with me in the back seat. I really needed my own identity. I was stuck in a routine that I did not plan for. My life was predetermined, and here I was just sitting in the back seat complacently, allowing someone else to take the steering wheel. I needed to take control again. I was tired of the predictability. I hated the predictability. In a sense, I had become a paradox, predictable in my unpredictability. I needed to let go and trust in myself.

I had to learn to embrace uncertainty. I had to learn that I could take my car off autopilot and drive the damn thing myself! I had to learn to be willing to take risks and push myself out of my amazingly comfortable zone. I had to learn that I would never change the things that I wanted to change in myself if I did not **believe** in myself and **believe** that I could make those changes I desired.

I had to learn to live with intention. I had to learn to live on purpose. I had to learn to put value on my own life. I had to learn to put value on what I valued and desired the most.

I formulated a plan of action and wrote my goals in my journal. I then read those goals every day.

My plan came together when I finally made the decision about what it was that I wanted most out of my life. I made a promise to myself then and there that I would be disciplined and be accountable for everything that I did from then on. Little steps get you the biggest rewards if you keep forging ahead, and do not look back. Every morning I made a promise to myself that I would keep working towards the changes that I wanted to accomplish that day. I also decided to take each day as it came, with the intention that I was going to make the changes necessary to get to my desired outcome. I decided to live my life on purpose.

"The more you trust your intuition, the more empowered you become, the stronger you become and the happier you become."

— GISELE BUNDCHEN

CHAPTER 7

"Be strong now because things will get better.
It might be stormy now,
but it can't rain forever."

— UNKNOWN

The entire world just received the biggest kick in the pants we have ever encountered.

The Coronavirus pandemic changed our lives in the blink of an eye when the year 2020 began. It seemed trivial to me to write about my personal change when the entire world had changed so rapidly. I needed to write about the pandemic, and how it changed every one of us. COVID-19 changed the world as we knew it just a short while ago.

Staying positive when faced with adversity:

We all have a choice; we can choose to face adversity with negative responses, or we can rise to the challenge by remaining positive. We can use this time to complain, or we can be resilient, positive, and motivated.

Life will always be tough. Every one of us will face misfortune and calamitous events in our lives at one time or another, such as what happened with the COVID-19 crisis. We can choose to hide our heads in the sand. We can pretend that what is happening around us will not happen to us personally, or we can be proactive and do what is required to help prevent a worsening situation for all of us.

We can choose to be negative, or we can choose to be positive and ready to do what we can to help fight this disaster. Adversity is a part of life. We can face that adversity and uncertainty with being strong and with a fighting spirit. Remember that we cannot control what is happening around us, but we can control our own thoughts and attitudes about it.

When life knocks us down, we have two choices. We can stay down, or we can get up and be a force to be reckoned with.

We will not be the same after this storm; we will be stronger.

Do not preoccupy your mind with how bad everything is. Occupy it with what you can do about it. Be grateful for what you have.

Extraordinary people survive under the worst conditions. **Be extraordinary**. It is in your power to do so.

It's your reaction to the adversity, not the adversity itself, that could break you. Challenge yourself to find the good in your situation and count your blessings. Be grateful for what you do have. Take each day as it comes. Focus on getting through each day by remaining positive. What will define us is how we react to the challenges facing us. Stay optimistic, because things will get better.

Take control of your own situation. Embrace the uncertainty and know there is always a rainbow after the storm.

We can choose to be part of the problem, or the solution. We can choose to care about our fellow humans, or we can choose to think solely about ourselves and buy up all the toilet paper and the hand sanitizer so there isn't enough left for the rest of us. We can clean out the meat departments in our local grocery stores, or we can remember that we must share with everyone to keep us all healthy.

Each one of us is completely responsible for our own behaviour.

Adversity can change our lives in the blink of an eye.

A true community is not just about being geographically close to our neighbors. It's about being connected and being responsible for the global community, as well as the communities that we live in.

Being socially and morally responsible means doing the right thing, and if that means closing all non-essential shops, businesses, and travel, then we must comply. If being socially responsible means we should be self-isolating and physically distant, then we must comply. It is our duty to help stop the spread of disease. We all must do what is needed to have a safe and healthy environment again.

Every one of us needs to accept responsibility for our actions. Morally we have a responsibility to help protect not only our families, but our fellow humans as well. There is no room for moral complacency and lack of responsibility in a crisis such as this.

We can overcome challenges by remembering our core values. We can help our neighbors and fellow humans by being kind, caring, and compassionate.

We all need to remember that it's not just during a pandemic that we need to do these things. We all need to learn a lesson from this global disaster, and remember to think of our fellow humans, not just ourselves.

When this pandemic is over, will the world be changed for the better? Will we all be able to work together afterward, as we have been doing during this crisis?

We are all in this crisis together.

Do you think that the Universe has sent us a stern warning that it was time for a change in the world as we knew it yesterday? Do you think the Universe needed to make us all so uncomfortable that we do not have a choice now?

No single person has figured everything out, but maybe collectively, if the world works together, we can make the changes that are needed.

We as humans have been creating separateness by judging others, when perhaps we simply are afraid to embrace others and live with love and compassion for our fellow humans.

Through all this adversity, can we not find peace and contentment with one another? Ours is not to judge, but to find ways to live together in the global community. By not cooperating, we have nothing to gain, and everything to lose. Nobody wins when we create fear and judge others. The truth is that we as a global community need to learn acceptance and to work together with everyone, no matter what race, color, or religion. We all need to have compassion for our fellow humans.

We will find our way through this crisis, and I believe that when we do, the world will be a better place.

"Too often we underestimate the power of a touch, a smile, a kind word, a listening ear, an honest compliment, or the smallest act of caring, all of which have the potential to turn a life around."

— LEO BUSCAGLIA

As I tore the March page off the calendar this morning, I thought about all the people that are alone.

Human connection is vital not only for our emotional health, but our physical health, as well.

Nothing is more apparent now than ever before that human touch is the basic of all needs. There is nothing that can heal human suffering more than the comfort of a human hand.

Sometimes words cannot express what a simple hug can do. A hug is energy that is passed from one to another through the act of touch. Hugs are essential for our wellbeing.

I grew up in a family of huggers. We hugged every morning before we went to school. We hugged when we visited our grandparents, aunts, and uncles. We hugged our friends, and our parents' friends. I watched not only my mother give hugs, but my macho father as well. He hugged his siblings and mother every time he saw them. He always had a hug for his children.

Studies have shown that hugs, hand holding, and massages reduce stress and can also boost the immune system. Touch is the first sense we develop in the womb. It is a fact that we have approximately five million touch receptors in our skin. There are three thousand of those touch receptors in our fingertips alone. Touch stimulates the release of endorphins, which is a natural painkiller.

All facts aside, every one of us needs physical touch. Right now, with what is happening in our world, the pandemic has made hugging and touching one another impossible. We as humans were never meant to hold one another at arm's length. We need physical contact. We need connection with one another. We need touch. We need hugs. Sometimes that hug is worth more than any words you could ever say.

CHAPTER 8

"If you believe it will work out,
you'll see opportunities. If you believe it won't,
you'll see obstacles."

— WAYNE DYER

Optimism is the ability to see the world around you with a positive outlook. Optimists expect that change will happen for the good.

If you are optimistic, it means you see opportunity in every situation, even if the situation is a difficult one. I heard a saying from my mother many years ago: **"A pessimist sees the dark clouds and cries; an optimist doesn't see the clouds, because she is walking on them."** She told me that I was an optimist. She also often told me to **"get my head out of the clouds and plant my feet firmly on the ground."**

Most of the time, I tend to see the best in everyone and everything. Now that I am older, I temper my optimism with realism. My mother also used to tell me to **"follow my heart, but take my brain with me."** Now I know she was telling me it was okay to be optimistic, but to add some reality to it. I did not really understand that as a child.

I see better things for the entire world especially after the crisis is over, and I do believe that it will soon be over. I would rather focus on the good than the negative that will come out of this disaster. Most of us tend to dwell on the bad things that have happened and could possibly still happen. I am looking to the good that will come out of this adversity.

There will be good to come out of this world situation. We may not see it in the immediate future because we will still be recovering, but we will see it happen. We have seen so much good during this disaster—people helping neighbors, different nations helping one another.

I am an optimist who's realistic enough to know and understand that not everything can be solved with optimism, and yet, I'm willing to try. I am not a defeatist. I believe that the crisis we are in will be solved and the world will be a far better place.

The defeatists are the ones who say the world has gone to shit, and nothing is going to change that. The realists are the ones who say we will have thousands of more deaths and many months of hard work to do before the world will be safe and free from COVID-19. The optimist in me says that we have already begun our recovery within a shorter time frame than was originally predicted. Soon we will have a vaccination, and other medical aids to halt this terrible disease.

The optimist in me believes that the world will be healed, and humans will have learned a valuable lesson. There are signs all over the world that we are healing. Today as I write this, there are fewer new cases of COVID-19. There are fewer deaths in many parts of the world. We are getting better at self-isolation. We are following the guidelines suggested by government health officials to halt the spread of this disease.

We cannot go back and change what happened. We can only go forward and learn from the past. We must all learn from our mistakes.

Remember in the blink of an eye, everything as you know it can be taken away. Be grateful for each day as it comes.

Open your eyes and your heart, and realize that life is good; you woke up this morning.

"Each of us has a fire in our heart for something. It's our goal in life to find it and keep it."

— MARY-LOU RETTON

CHAPTER 9

"Hope is important because it can make the present moment less difficult to bear. If we believe that tomorrow will be better, we can bear a hardship today."

— THICH NHAT HANH

Lately, over the past few weeks, I have been hearing from others how their emotions have been different from day to day.

Sometimes they feel positive and uplifted. Often, they felt anxious and overwhelmed. Other times they were perplexed, disturbed, and emotionally drained. Sometimes they felt anger, discouragement and even panic over the impact that this crisis is having over the world.

I thought I was immune to these negative feelings because I had trained my mind to see the positive in every situation, and I could feel gratitude for even the smallest things in my life.

I was mistaken.

Over the last few days, I fell prey to negative feelings and deep distress. I felt dismay that I had not seen my family for months. I felt anger over not being able to do the things that were important to me. I was upset that I did not have my job to go to, because all the shops had been closed.

I was finding it extremely difficult to snap myself out of these debilitating feelings. I felt immense alarm for the future. I have been in self-isolation for over a month now, and I am desperate for human connection and interaction.

This is what I wrote in my journal on April 6, 2020:

Yesterday is history.

Today I awoke with a different attitude. My first thought on awakening at 3:49 am was, "Today I am alive, I am healthy, and I am grateful. I am grateful for all that I do have."

You see, your thoughts are immensely powerful. Just one positive thought when you awaken each morning can set the tone for the entire day. I am not saying that you must be a Pollyanna. Being positive does not mean that you must find the good in every day if you cannot see it; it simply means that you know that things will get better eventually. Tomorrow will be a better day, and the day after that will be better still, and so on.

I reminded myself to stop stressing over what I was unable to control, and to concentrate only on what I could control. I can control my feelings. I can control my thoughts. I reminded myself about my beautiful surroundings: the beach, the forest, and the snow-capped mountains that I have the good fortune to see every day. I reminded myself that I am healthy. I have a roof over my head. I have food, and I have time to do the things that I have been wanting to do.

I have each day of the rest of my life to look forward to. I have hope, and faith.

I know deep in my heart that everything will work out for the best. Life will go on—maybe not exactly as before, but it will go on. I believe there is a better world out there. We all just need to embrace our circumstances and know in our hearts that things will get better.

"Realize that true happiness lies within you.
Waste no time and effort searching for peace
and contentment and joy in the world outside.
Remember that there is no happiness in having
joy in getting but only in giving.
Reach out. Share. Smile. Hug.
Happiness is a perfume you cannot pour on
others without a few drops on yourself."

— OG MANDINO

CHAPTER 10

> "I don't have to chase extraordinary moments to find happiness—it's right in front of me, if I'm paying attention and practicing gratitude."
>
> — BRENE BROWN

I love watching the daylight sneak into the dark that the night leaves behind in the early morning hours. It slowly wipes the blackness away and gives us another reason to begin a new day free from the encumbrances of yesterday. Free from despair and worry. It gives us another beginning, another chance to make a difference. Our lives might be in limbo right now, but that does not give us a reason to be unhappy and miserable with our lives.

A new day gives us hope and an opportunity to kick butt! If yesterday was difficult, concentrate on changing your attitude about everything. Change your attitude if you cannot change the situation. Concentrate on making today the best day of your life. Use the best dinnerware, the crystal goblets and the best silverware. Set it all up on the best tablecloth. Treat each day as a celebration.

All we have is today. Yesterday is in the past; leave it there. That is where it belongs. It does not belong in your mind to be gone over again and again. Let it go! What happened yesterday is no longer of any importance. Do not let the memories of yesterday ruin your opportunities to make today the best damn day of your life.

Concentrate only on the things that you can do to make today better! You will never get today back again.

As a matter of fact, with even a tiny adjustment in your attitude, you **can** make this the best day of your life. Just spend a few minutes being grateful for everything that you have. Remember all those things that you are thankful for.

I am thankful for opening my eyes another day. I am thankful I have people in my life that love me. I am grateful for the people that I can love back. I am grateful that I am healthy. I am grateful for all the amazing and wonderful people that I have in my life who support me.

I am incredibly grateful for the person I am today.

The power behind being grateful is like an instant pick-me-up. I promise with just a tiny adjustment in how you look at everything, your day will be better. Being grateful gives you a happy heart. When your heart is happy, you can appreciate life, even when it's not perfect.

"Let yourself be silently drawn by
the strange pull of what you really love.
It will not lead you astray."

— RUMI

CHAPTER 11

"For my part, I travel not to anywhere,
but to go. I travel for travel's sake.
The great affair is to move."

— ROBERT LOUIS STEVENSON

One of the things that I miss most at the present time is traveling. Over the past several years, I finally began to do the things that I have always wanted to do. Traveling was one of those desires that I had for many years, but was unable to do because of various excuses that I would come up with: *I couldn't afford it. I had no one to travel with, or a destination. I was afraid to travel alone.* Just excuse after excuse.

Several years ago, I had finally realized my desire to travel, and I have had many enjoyable trips by myself.

Now I cannot think of anything that excites me more than traveling. Traveling alone is one of the most exhilarating and liberating experiences I have ever had.

Sometimes you just need an adventure to clear the mind and the soul. Traveling makes me happy and gives me the freedom that I have been missing for years. I think I may have been born with the soul of a nomad. Sometimes I just need an adventure. Travel is therapy for me.

During the pandemic, I was suffering from *no-trip-a-phobia—the fear of not having any trips booked.

Life is meant for great adventures. Traveling alone means you are completely responsible for yourself and it is then you realize just how capable you are.

Life is a journey, so why not use your journey to discover new places and people? Traveling is not just about the result; it is about what you do and who you meet along the way. Traveling is far more about the journey than the destination.

I prefer to fill my life with experiences rather than stuff now. I am finally living my dreams. I love airports and airplanes. I love the feeling of arriving someplace that is new to me. I love discovering and meeting new people.

We live in a world filled with wonder and beauty. There is no end to the adventures we can have.

I have learned to take every opportunity that I can in life now, because if I don't, the opportunity will be lost. My mother used to say, "**Make hay while the sun shines.**" I know now what she meant: take advantage of opportunities presented to you, or they will be gone forever.

I know that soon I will be traveling again. Soon the world will heal and be well. The adventures will be there for me, and I will be ready for them.

I will follow my heart. I will be a *rebel on purpose.*

"You have brains in your head. You have feet in your shoes. You can steer yourself any direction you choose."

— DR. SEUSS

CHAPTER 12

> "This will pass... and when it does, you'll be stronger that you ever thought you could be."
>
> — KRISTEN BUTLER

Most of us have been in self-isolation for months now. By now, most of us are ready for some human contact other than Zoom meetings, FaceTime, and virtual hugs. We are all looking forward to spending time with family and friends. We are all taking it one day at a time.

I think we surprised ourselves that we made it this far without going a little crazy. Keeping ourselves at home and staying away from gatherings is not easy.

Most of us, when we do have to venture out for groceries and work, have been able to keep to the 2 metre or 6-foot rule of staying away from other people. I see many with masks and gloves just to make sure they are staying safe and healthy, and keeping everyone else healthy and safe as well.

Our world as we knew it has been changed forever. I do believe that we will look back on this time and realize that we learned a great deal. We learned that we could survive in a crisis.

The thing is that most of us have been able to survive this disaster with the knowledge that we can begin again. Business will go on; our lives will go on. We will be stronger.

We all have the power within us to affect the changes that we desire. We can become better human beings if we have the desire to change.

We have learned that we do not need to see the entire road ahead of us. We do not need to have it all figured out. There can be some unexpected twists and turns, and we will still come through it all with grace and grit.

Many of us have learned that we are indeed warriors. We have chosen to not give up when facing adversity. We have learned that what we want is worth fighting for. We have learned that we can overcome this hardship that has hit us in the gut with both fists.

Life and love are beautiful gifts, and we cannot ever take them for granted.

We need to embrace the changes and learn to live our lives to the fullest. We never know when we will breathe our last breath. Better things are coming. Yesterday's troubles are just that; yesterday's troubles.

We will survive this adversity. Life will be good again, and we will need the energy and the mindset to change with the times.

The truth is that we can change our lives at any time we wish. We can do whatever we want to do.

We all have the power within us to affect whatever changes we desire.

> "I believe in pink. I believe that laughing is the best calorie burner. I believe in kissing, kissing a lot. I believe in being strong when everything seems to be going wrong. I believe that happy girls are the prettiest. I believe that tomorrow is another day, and I believe in miracles."
>
> — AUDREY HEPBURN

I believe in miracles; I believe that tomorrow will be a better day. I believe in being strong when everything is going wrong. I believe in being grateful for every day that has passed. I believe in being grateful for every day that is before us. We will be okay. We will survive and be stronger. We all need to be more appreciative for the little things. We will find more happiness in doing our daily routines again when we do.

CHAPTER 13

> "Life doesn't come with a manual. It comes with a mother."
>
> — UNKNOWN

Most of us are still self-isolating, social distancing and being careful about large gatherings.

I like to go for a walk nearly every day to clear my mind and think about things other than the pandemic and its effect on everyone in this world.

I like to walk along the beach, or along the numerous walking trails in our little paradise here on Vancouver Island.

I came across a sign along the path the other day while trying to think of something to post for Mother's Day. "Please slow down, baby ducklings crossing path." I was hoping to see the baby ducklings that day, but they were nowhere to be seen.

Remembering that sign made me think about mothers.

One of my greatest supporters was my mother. She was an amazingly patient woman. She had four children with me as the eldest, and she worked while maintaining a home and four kids. I often wished I had her patience, even just a little bit of it. It's something that I work on every day.

Having a mom who worked outside the home every day meant that I, as the eldest, had to take on many duties that were required of the wife and mother back then.

After school, I was elected to pick up my baby brother from the sitter's. I had to make sure my other siblings got safely home from school. I had to get them settled at the kitchen table to do their homework before they could go outside to play.

I had to make sure dinner would be ready and on the table for when my dad came home from work. My mother usually came home a little after he arrived.

Then I had to do the clean up because *men did not do those things then,* and mom was usually too exhausted to after work. She always let me know how much she appreciated my efforts, though. I think that was when I began to think that all women were supposed to be supermoms; work all day, and still keep a spotless home and dinner on the table for when their husbands came home from work.

I always tried my best to be like her. It took me many years to realize that I needed to be me and not my mother, or the image of who I thought she was.

Even still, I loved my mom dearly, and learned a lot from her.

Thank God for mothers. They are the strengths of this world.

"What you notice, give attention to,
talk about, get all worked up over emotionally
is what you are inviting into your life,
whether you mean to or not."

— CATHERINE PONDER

CHAPTER 14

> "Opportunities to find deeper powers within ourselves come when life seems most challenging."
>
> — JOSEPH CAMPBELL

Although we have been going through a very frightening experience, many of us have been able to cope quite well. Most of us have been able to slow down and spend more time with family, doing the things that we know are important, but never seemed to be able to make time for before. We have learned that people do get stronger in times of hardships, like what we are experiencing now. Awareness has opened our eyes to the rest of the world. We are all connected because of this pandemic.

This much I do know: we are all so much stronger than we thought we were. Every challenge that we are faced with will only make us stronger than we have ever been before. Keep reminding yourself that these obstacles that have been placed on our way are just steppingstones to help us grow. We do not grow when things are easy and just handed to us. We grow when things are tough, and we are faced with demanding situations and adversity.

Even though we do not have any control over what is happening in the world right now, we do have control over how we handle all of it within ourselves. We always have control over our responses and our mind set. By simply changing the wording from "we are all stuck at home" to "we are all safe at home," can change the entire way we respond to our situation every day.

There will always be challenging situations to face. The greatest lessons we learn during our lifetime will come from adversity. The challenges that we face are what makes up our life and gives it meaning.

Keeping calm and positive during this unprecedented and unfortunate time is essential to our peace of mind.

> "Hardships often prepare ordinary people for an extraordinary outcome."
>
> — C.S. LEWIS

Our world was invaded by a new enemy, and we learned how to fight back without violence. We learned how to fight back by being cooperative and productive. We learned how to be resilient. We learned how to join forces and collaborate with others over social media. We learned to love our fellow humans.

Canada is preparing to slowly lessen restrictions as the Coronavirus cases begin to decrease. It is a reminder that we will get through this crisis eventually. We still have a long way to go, but we will get there.

We have all gone through this traumatic experience, and many of us have become much stronger. Some of us came out with a new skill; some with more knowledge. Many of us made good use of our isolation time to learn something new. Many of us used this time to connect over social media with family that we have not seen or heard from for years. Some of us simply learned new coping skills.

Many of us learned to take a step back and re-evaluate our lives. Self-improvement became the thing to do for many. *Stay healthy, stay safe, stay positive, be kind and remain calm* became the buzzwords. We learned that some things are out of our control. Most of us learned to accept that so we could survive emotionally. We learned to be grateful for every day that we remained healthy.

We learned that family and friendships are what is most important in our lives, not material things. We learned to embrace change. We learned to be patient. We learned to embrace the uncertainty and plan for the future. We learned that the life in front of us will be far better than the one we are leaving behind.

We learned we all had to take massive determined action. No one person in the world escaped some kind of involvement in this crisis.

We learned that we had to have faith that the world will heal, but we also learned that we had to put action behind that faith. We all had to work toward making our world healthy again.

The message was loud and clear; each day is a gift to be cherished and lived to the fullest.

"Everything will work out in the end.
You don't need to know how.
You just have to trust that it will."

— LIVE LIFE HAPPY

Often when we go through traumatic events, we have a difficult time seeing the light at the end of the tunnel. Seeing through this adversity becomes even more difficult the longer we are faced with it.

We need to decide for ourselves that everything will work out in the end. We do not need to have all the answers. We simply need to make ourselves understand that things will eventually work out. Life does have a way of working out the way it is supposed to after all.

I subscribe to the fact that everything does happen for a reason. Sometimes that reason is not quite apparent as with COVID-19 and the many illnesses and deaths that it has caused. I know that right now life seems to be headed in the wrong direction. In reality though, it is going the right way. Even if things do not feel good for a while, and even if it feels like things will never be okay again, everything will work out in the end. It might take a year or maybe two, but things will get better. Your attitude during this adverse time will determine your strengths to get through this hardship.

Don't focus on what is missing; focus only on the fact that everything will be okay in the end.

NO TRESPASS

"What you lack in talent can be made up with desire, hustle and giving 110% all the time."

— Don Zimmer

CHAPTER 15

"When circumstances are out of your control, remember you are in control of how you respond."

— LINDA BREEDLOVE

This will be my last chapter about the COVID-19 pandemic. Not because it's over, but because we could keep rehashing it over and over again, and we will still come up with all the same questions and the same answers. We come up with the same predictions and problems every time.

This monstrosity will not go away until a vaccine is discovered.

Sometimes it seems like the chaos in the world will never end. It just keeps beating down on us like a tornado that will not stop twisting its way through the countryside—only this tornado is twisting its way through the entire world. The things that we worried about pre-pandemic seemed trivial while this crisis is happening.

Everyone in the entire world is affected in some way. We need to remember that we are not alone in this storm.

We will never forget this time in our lives. We will never forget about all the people that lost their lives because of this virus. We will never forget the heroes that made a difference.

Someday everything will make sense again. Our lives will go on. Maybe our lives won't go on quite as before, but we will go on. Living through a pandemic has made us realize that it is the little things that matter. Family and friends have become far more important than we ever thought.

We have felt overwhelmed. We have felt terrified. We have felt panicked and frightened for the future. There was no getting away from our fears. We discovered that it is easier to feel positive and motivated when things are going well, but we have found that it is so much more difficult to keep those positive thoughts when things are going bad. We must work harder at making ourselves hold our heads above the incoming tide. For myself, I found that even though I keep writing about keeping positive and motivated, I too had to work at it daily to make myself believe in what I was saying. Not one of us has escaped the turmoil within and the reminders every day that we are in the midst of a world crisis.

We have learned that life is fragile. But we have learned that humans are very resilient and stronger than we thought they were. We have learned that this life is a privilege, and we should be grateful for all that we have. We have learned to take each day as it comes and to live in the present.

> "Resilience is not just for surviving the worst day of your life. It's for thriving every day of your life."
>
> — DR. RICK HANSON.

Resilience: the capacity to recover from difficulties.

Nothing is more necessary than the need to recover from adversity. To recover from adversity, you need to be resilient.

An example of resilience is this; I had planted a beautiful purple clematis many years ago, but I planted it too close to a honeysuckle vine which was taking over the area. The clematis always had to fight to take its rightful place in the garden, and never really had a chance. During a tree removal, it had gotten stomped on and decimated. I thought it was finally gone because it did not grow and bloom that year or the next. Well, this year during the Coronavirus pandemic, it unexpectedly decided to grow again. It not only grew, but produced more huge purple blossoms than ever before. That plant showed me resilience.

The resilience of that plant also made me realize we never know how much strength and resiliency we have in us.

When life slaps us in the face, it's time to wake up and discover our capabilities. Going through hardships is not a permanent state. We may not be able to control everything that happens in our lives, but we can control our own minds and reactions to that hardship.

The adversity we faced during the pandemic or any other adverse time in our lives will not stop us. We will not give in. We can and will endure many setbacks in our lives. We have deep roots, and we will grow again.

We will not just survive; we will thrive.

We are all warriors, and we are fighting back against the odds.

Things might get tough, but we are tougher. We have power over our minds. We humans are a resilient race. We are a resilient world. We are all able to roll with the punches if we choose to. We are not victims. We should not behave like victims. We are tough and hardy like the clematis, even when we do not think we are.

Life will not get any easier for us; we will simply get stronger, and we will bounce back.

The struggles we face do not define us. Those struggles will be our strengths for tomorrow.

CHAPTER 16

"Self-discipline starts with the mastery of your thoughts. If you don't control what you think, you can't control what you do."

— NAPOLEON HILL

Discipline versus motivation:

Motivation comes from the emotional part of your thoughts. Motivation is positive. It gives you reasons to carry on with attaining your dreams and desires when you sometimes feel like quitting. Motivation always begins with your dreams. You must first have the desire, and then you can work on motivating yourself to get it. Motivation is the desire to do what it is that you want to do. Motivation, though, is only part of your desires and dreams. Staying motivated is not always easy.

Abraham Lincoln said, "Discipline is choosing between what you want now, and what you want most."

Motivation is not always in your control. Discipline though is strictly within your control.

Discipline is reason. Discipline is also the negative part of success. Discipline is only the way to successfully attain your dreams and desires. Motivation will not take you anywhere; you must have the discipline to carry through with what it is that you want the most. You must master your thoughts and decide what it is that you really want. Discipline is the only way to make yourself do the things that are required to finish your goal. Most people, though they are motivated, are not disciplined enough to carry something through the finish line.

Discipline is where I have the greatest difficulty. I had to train myself to be disciplined, and I must work at keeping discipline every day, even though I know that being disciplined is the only way I will get to my desired result.

Discipline is making yourself do the things required to attain your goal. Discipline is reason. Discipline is making yourself sit down at the computer and write every day. Discipline is making yourself accountable for what it is that you desire the most.

Discipline is making yourself do something, even when you do not feel like doing it.

When I knew I had to lose weight, I was genuinely motivated to do it; motivation worked for a while. When it became mundane to stick to my new weight loss plan, I had to discipline myself to keep going. No matter how I was feeling, or no matter how many times that I wanted to quit, I knew that I had to keep going. I had to keep the finish line in focus, and be disciplined enough to keep going towards my goal.

Discipline is putting the action behind your motivation. Discipline is the only way you will succeed in your goal. Without discipline, I would not have written my first book. I would not have lost the weight I wanted. Without discipline, I would not have grown to be who I am today.

Discipline takes practice and willpower. It takes consistency. It takes being in control of your desires, and in knowing what desires are most important to you. Your life is one hundred percent your responsibility. Commit to your dreams, and be disciplined enough to see them through to being fulfilled. Do what needs to be done. Make your desires a priority. Live your life on purpose, and with intent.

> "People of accomplishment rarely sat back and let things happen to them. They went out and happened to things."
>
> — LEONARDO DA VINCI

People who accomplish great things do not just sit back and wait for them to happen. They go out and make them happen. Sometimes things will get difficult. Sometimes those things will seem insurmountable. However, I believe we are all stronger than we realize. I believe we all have it in us to accomplish our greatest desires. I believe that we should wake up every morning with the mindset that today will be the best day of our life, and we will accomplish our goals.

I have heard people say, "I don't have time to go after my dreams." Well I have news for those people. We all have the same amount of time. We all have twenty-four hours in the day to do what we desire. I believe that lack of motivation and direction is the problem for some. I have been guilty of that as well. I was content to just let every day slide by without working on my goals and dreams.

I thought I had to just let things happen. Boy, was I wrong! Life is not about waiting for things to happen; life is about making them happen. All I had to do was make the decision to act on my dreams and desires.

I had to do more than simply just exist. I had to learn that life passes you by if you do not act. I had to dream my biggest dream, and I had to work hard to attain it. I knew that if I continually worried about what I wanted to do, that I would never go anywhere. I learned that I had to leave my worries behind and concentrate on the result, and what it was that I desired the most.

So what if I failed? So what if I figured out that believing in myself made it possible to make my dreams come true? If I failed, so what! At least I did what I wanted to do, and I could use it as a learning experience. You only really fail if you stop trying.

There are two women in my life right now who have inspired me greatly. I will call one "S," and the other one "R." Both women went after their dreams and showed me that if you genuinely believe in yourself, you can be successful. Both women have shown that with determination and an abundance of grace (and a smattering of grit), you can have what you want. Both have failed in the past. Both got up and tried again. Failure was not an option for them. These two women have shown me that with the right attitude and determination, you can be who you want to be, and do what you want to do.

I followed my heart and it led me to a place I never knew existed. It led me right to happiness and contentment. I learned that my dreams could come true; I only needed to find the courage to pursue them.

"Be the kind of woman who,
when your feet hit the floor in the morning, the Devil says, 'Oh no, she's up!'"

— UNKNOWN

"For surely we become like the things in which we believe. Our thoughts make us what we are. We take on the characteristics of our convictions."

— MARCUS BACH

CHAPTER 17

"Strength does not come from physical capacity. It comes from an indomitable will."

— MAHATMA GHANDI

We all have a power within us to affect the change we desire. Our minds are far more powerful than we think they are.

When you accept responsibility for all that you are, you will have the power to change what it is that you desire to change. Whatever you believe in your mind will happen for you if your belief is strong and your desire is there, followed by discipline to keep going in the direction of the change you want.

Decide what you want and believe that you can have it. Believe that you deserve it. Believe that it's possible for you. **Believe**. Keep that belief strong and focus on it with intent to do it. Focus on it constantly, and repeat that desire over and over; eventually, your subconscious mind will accept it.

Sigmund Freud equates our minds to an iceberg. We use only ten percent of our minds consciously; the other ninety percent is our subconscious. It is in our subconscious minds where we will find our purpose. The more we know ourselves, the more we can accomplish. The more we repeat to ourselves what it is that we desire, the more our subconscious minds will accept it as truth.

You must remember that your desire to change what you want to change in yourself must be stronger than your desire to remain as you are. If you have found your passion and desire it strong enough, then make the changes that are necessary. Be brave and do the things that challenge you. Demand the change from yourself. Get excited about what you want, and just go for it!

Remember you are worth every effort you make on yourself. Do not underestimate yourself. You are a force to be reckoned with. Do not ever give up on yourself. Sometimes you just need to ignore the doubt. You just need to ignore logic. Forget about the complications. You need to just go for it.

Strength does not come from the things that you can do. Strength comes from overcoming the things that you thought you could not do. If something seems too difficult, it does not mean that what you want to do is impossible. It simply means that you must work harder to do it.

Take a deep breath, and stop being afraid. Either it will work out or you will have learned a lesson from it. Do not waste your time or your life wondering if you would have succeeded or failed, for if you did not go for it, you have failed. You have failed yourself.

"Don't count the days, make the days count."

— MUHAMMAD ALI

CHAPTER 18

> "There is a fountain of youth; it is your mind, your talents, the creativity you bring to your life and the lives of people you love. When you learn to tap into this source, you will have truly defeated age."
>
> — SOPHIA LOREN

I do not believe in using age as an excuse to get old.

Recently I sat listening to an acquaintance complain that nothing exciting happened in her life anymore. She said that she was too old to enjoy the things that she used to love doing, and she could not physically do some of the things she used to love to do.

What she said could not be further from the truth. Getting older is not the issue. We all must "grow older." We do not have to accept age as the end though. We do not have to accept that our age must stop us from enjoying our lives. Age is only the number of years we have lived on this earth. I believe that the number of years we have behind us has no bearing on how old we are. I strongly believe that we are only as old as our attitudes about our age.

Our age is not a barrier to doing the activities that we want to do. It's the limitations that we put into our minds that can stop us from enjoying the experiences that we could be having. Age does not define who we are. How we handle our aging is the only thing that defines us. It's all in our attitudes.

Recently, on one of my solo trips while waiting for my flight, an older gentleman and I struck up a friendly conversation. During that conversation, he told me he was 90 years old, and he recently had open heart surgery. He had snow gear with him, and he was heading to a ski resort to do some snowboarding with his son. He told me that he learned to snowboard quite late in his life. It worried him that after his heart surgery, he may not be able to snowboard again. After his recovery, he worked hard to prove to himself that he could do it again. He was so excited about getting out snowboarding again, and he was not letting his heart, or his age interfere with his goals. His enthusiasm to be back on his snowboard on the snowy mountains was inspiring.

We can decide to have many regrets and live in the past, or we can decide to live every day before us with the same fervour that we had when we were 20.

Lack of enthusiasm is what ages us. Bring that enthusiasm back into your life, and you will feel younger and more vibrant than ever. Make the decision to be healthy and stay active. Never stop dreaming and never stop believing. Make an impact right now with your life. Appreciate that you are now wiser than you were at 20. Appreciate that you are, "old enough to know better, and young enough to do it again."

There is a privilege to becoming older. You find out more about yourself. You find out that what other people think of you no longer matters. You realize that you can simply walk away from situations that are not conducive to your wellbeing and peace of mind. You realize that you and only you are responsible for your decisions. You realize that you cannot put the blame on anyone else for who you are, and what you have become. You still have time to be the person you have always wanted to be.

I like to tell people that I finally found out what I wanted to be when I grew up. I finally became the rebel that was always just festering beneath the surface just itching to get out.

Wear that sexy lingerie! Wear those tight jeans! Quit reading those articles that tell you what to wear and how to behave after

50. Do something that you have only dreamed about doing. Go snowboarding, go zip lining, go skydiving, travel solo, find a lover. Do what you have a desire to do. Be that badass you have always wanted to be. Stop acting old. **Be a Rebel.** Embrace the journey of your life. You have many years in front of you to do exactly what you have been dreaming of doing.

CHAPTER 19

"Embrace the journey—be a rebel on purpose."

— LINDA BREEDLOVE

I have been using social media for several years now to post various messages—usually positive and motivational ones. That was how I acquired the material for my first book. I realised that my posts were helping other women and men become more cognizant of the fact that they too could live life with more happiness and contentment than what they were experiencing now in their lives.

I have the wonderful good fortune of having one of these people as a friend (I will call her "C.") C is a beautiful woman. She has been blessed with a wonderful family, including grandchildren. She is amazing in the fact that she is always trying to make improvements with her life. She has a husband who has been living with cancer for several years now. C has been working extremely hard at keeping herself as positive as possible during these unfortunate circumstances mostly to help him through his illness.

Recently, she messaged me with a few questions about a social media post that I did about motivation and enthusiasm. These are her words: *"Morning! Thanks so much for your message this morning—very powerful. I am wondering how much your weight loss had to do with your journey. Did your journey pick up after your weight loss, or did the weight loss come as part of the journey? There was a lot in your post. Motivation and enthusiasm are in short supply at the moment. I wake up with it every day, then it fades away. Also, being a people pleaser my entire life, I really don't know who I am or what I want to do anymore. I copied your message into my notes and have read it several times already. C."*

I had to think about my answer to her for a few hours. I wanted to be noticeably clear in my response. This is my response to her:

"Dear C, your questions and remarks this morning gave me a lot to think about. I don't think I ever thought about when my transformation really began until I received your message this morning.

I think that I must have made the decision to transform myself long before the weight loss. The weight loss was a result of the deep desire within me to make many changes in my mind, my body, and my soul.

I felt that I was always on the outside looking in. I felt that I did not really belong anywhere.

All I know is that I had this deep burning desire within me to make a difference, and I knew I had to start with myself. I changed my mindset to reflect the deep desires I had. When I changed my mindset, I began to see that the happiness and contentment I desired had to begin with me. I had to passionately believe it in my mind, and feel it in my heart first. I had to search deep within myself and tell myself the truth, even if it hurt a bit. Motivation and enthusiasm are only a small part of making changes in yourself. The biggest key is in the discipline. I had to discipline myself to just begin with small changes. It did not matter if I only took small steps every day; it only mattered that I kept going.

The weight loss definitely gave me the strength and the courage to keep going. Once I began to like myself better, I began to gather more strength to keep going. I began to like how I looked, and how I felt. I gained the self-esteem and the confidence back that I had lost so long ago. It used to matter what people thought of me, and now I do not worry about anything as trivial as that. It took me a while to reach that stage, though.

I understand what you mean by being a "people pleaser." My whole life was based on pleasing everyone else around me first, before myself. As a matter of fact, I don't remember pleasing myself with anything but food before. Now I please myself first, and it isn't with food. I buy a new book, or get a pedicure, or a facial, or a new outfit. I wake up happy and grateful every day for everything that I do have in my life.

I am no Pollyanna though. I still have some days that I feel down, or I do not feel like being positive and motivated. Now though, I know how to snap myself out of those bad thoughts. I just think about all the good that I have now. Writing my books has been one of the ways that I am able to change my negative thoughts into positive ones. I write my negative feelings down, and then, when I read what I have written, I realize how trivial they all are. I realize that I am on the receiving end of so much love and support from so many people in my life, and I feel completely uplifted. I am incredibly grateful for the support that I get from the amazing men and women that I have in my life now.

Take care of yourself first, C. You cannot drink from an empty cup."

CHAPTER 20

> "Fortunate is he who does not carry envy as a companion."
>
> — RUMI

Envy: the state of wishing we had something that another person has.

People that are envious of others feel like their world is not as wonderful or successful as others. They spend their time wishing they had a better life, more money, better clothes, better standing in their careers, etc. Envy is a negative emotion and is very destructive to your own mind and self esteem.

Instead of working on themselves to attain a better life, better job, or more happiness, people that are envious would rather sit back and be jealous of everyone else. Envy is born out of insecurities, lack of confidence, and a poor sense of self-worth.

Envy will reduce your ability to dream your own dreams and set your own goals.

Your power comes when you understand your own insecurities and jealousies to find out more about your own self. Realize what it is that is holding you back and work on getting rid of those doubts.

I used to be a little envious of the successful women around me, and wondered why I could not be more like them. That was my ego getting in the way. I finally admitted to myself that being envious was self-destructive and making me miserable. I finally clued into the fact that I could use that negative energy to motivate myself to become a better person.

When I did all of that, I found that I was no longer envious of successful people, and found myself on the road to making positive changes in myself. Envy comes from a lack of confidence in one's own abilities, and a lack of belief that they too can be successful.

I had years of feeling inferior, and I no longer felt inferior when I began to believe in myself. I learned to appreciate my own abilities and I understood that each of us is unique. Each of us has something to give that is different from everyone else.

I learned to be comfortable with myself, and my self-esteem grew. I learned to stop comparing myself to others and believe in the uniqueness of myself. When you stop comparing yourself to others, you find happiness and contentment in your life. I made the changes that I wanted to make in myself, and I am continuing to make changes that I want to make. True confidence comes when you embrace your own journey and know that your journey is your own special contribution to life.

If you have feelings of envy, take ownership of that fact and start believing in yourself. Make a list of all the beautiful and fantastic things you have in your life and be grateful for all that you have while working towards attaining more. Learn to accept who and what you are, while working towards what you desire to be.

Count your own blessings, for you have many. Learn appreciation for everything. Learn to admire someone else's worth without devaluing your own. True confidence comes when you stop comparing your life to someone else's. Live your best life, always. Support others and be happy for others who are doing well without letting your insecurities get in the way.

You will soon realize that envy has no place in your life.

"Everything that is created begins in the mind."

— RUTH FISHEL

CHAPTER 21

> "Serenity is not freedom from the storm, but peace amid the storm."
>
> — UNKNOWN

The ocean is like a magnet to me. Whenever something is on mind and I cannot seem to make sense of it or get it out of my mind, I head to my favourite place: the beach.

I wish everyone reading this right now was able to breathe in the scents of the ocean and hear the gentle sounds that I experience when I am at my happy place on the beach.

It is at the beach that I often find the answers that I am searching for... or at the very least, I can put the subject matter out of my mind and simply focus on the sounds, the smells, and the beauty of the ocean. It is there that I can put things into perspective. It is there that I take a deep breath of the clean crisp air, and realize that I can change what I want to change within myself. It is there that I know I can face any challenge put before me. It is there where I can make a promise to myself to change the things that I want to change.

The ocean itself has many moods; it can be stormy and difficult, or it can be calm and serene. Either way, there is always something beautiful to be found there.

Sometimes all one needs to calm the mind and open the heart is to spend a little time simply watching and listening to the waves roll over the sand and rocks.

Sometimes, it's all one needs to calm the storm within yourself.

Finding peace within yourself is paramount to finding your purpose. You must be happy with yourself and be grateful for what you have while searching for your purpose.

I know everyone doesn't have a beach to sit at to find the peace within themselves, but there are many other places you could go to. I recommend going alone to a favorite place to spend time thinking and pondering your purpose.

Find your happy place.

"Respond, don't react. Listen, don't talk.
Think, don't assume."

— RAJII LUKKOOR

Do you ever react instead of responding?

I am ashamed to say that recently I was faced with a situation where I reacted instead of responded. I was stopped at a red light when suddenly, I was hit from behind—rear-ended. My beautiful little convertible!

Now, anyone that knows me at all knows how much I love my BMW convertible. I was so shocked and upset that when I got out of my car to look, instead of responding in a calm manner, I reacted with anger. "How could you run into me like that? How could you hit my beautiful little convertible?" I took it as a personal insult. Instead of responding in a calm manner, I reacted! Bad choice!

I wrote about reacting instead of responding in my book, ***EMBRACE the CHANGE, Be a Rebel on Purpose.*** I KNOW that reacting is wrong!

I am sharing this with you, my readers, to let you know that we are all human, and we all make mistakes.

The ladies that hit me were exceedingly kind and caring. Because of their empathy I knew I had to calm myself down. I realized that sometimes shit happens. I took a deep breath and apologized for my sudden reactive and unkindly behaviour. It was just a car; I was not hurt, and neither were they. They were just as shocked as I was.

I am convinced that most of the reason I was upset was because I *allowed* myself to react instead of respond.

It comes down to choice again. We choose our responses. When we react, we have lost control over the situation. When we respond in a calm manner, we regain control.

In every situation, we have a choice: respond, or react. We cannot let any situation move us away from our source of power. Choose your reactions carefully. Choose control over loss of control. Always push your pause button when faced with a situation, any situation, and think before you utter anything.

I learned a valuable lesson that day. Life is 10% of what happens to you, and 90% of how you react or respond to it. Always be open to learning about yourself, because that is where your power is. If you make a mistake, be ready to correct it. Understand your own emotions, and be prepared to manage them with dignity when you falter. Do not be afraid to admit when you are wrong. Reframe your own behaviours and understand them, so you can handle any situation better and with class.

CHAPTER 22

"Balance is the key to everything.
What we do, think, say, eat, feel…
they all require awareness, and through this
awareness, we can grow."

— KOI FRESCO

Balance is not about fitting everything into your life. Balance is about doing the important things, and not worrying about the rest. It's about knowing that you cannot do all of it.

It took me a long time to get that! I did not understand how to live a balanced life. I was the type of person that threw herself into whatever it was that was consuming my life at the time. Work, family and homelife took all my attention. I thought that I had to please everyone else before pleasing myself. I thought that to do a great job with any of these, I had to immerse myself completely. That left no time for me.

It took me a long time to finally realize that I mattered too. Finding balance is necessary for a healthy mind and body. When you do not balance your life, you lose yourself in the process. The first thing to remember is to never compare yourself to anyone else. No two people are alike. Know what you can do, and give yourself credit for all that you do. Focus only on what you can control and let go of the rest.

Remember that you do not always have to be busy; you are allowed to rest. You don't always have to be the strong one. You do not always have to do it all. The biggest mountain you must climb is in your mind. You do not always need to do it all. It's okay to sometimes be a priority in your own life.

Balance will come if you pause in your pursuit, take a good look at your life, and realize that you do not have to control everything. Let go of the illusion that you must be perfect. You are allowed to just let some things happen.

I learned that I needed to take time for myself. I had to let go of the thinking that I had to control everything. I had to learn to just relax. I had to remember that I mattered too. I had to learn to prioritize my activities and responsibilities. I had to learn to delegate. I had to learn that perfection is not necessary. I had to learn to let go of what I perceived to be important, and understand that I was important, too.

It's okay to fail sometimes. It's okay to take one step at a time. It's okay to take things slowly. I had to learn to accept the journey, and not worry about the destination.

I had to learn that balance is necessary for not only a healthy mind, but also a healthy body.

"The more you trust your intuition, the more empowered you become, the stronger you become, and the happier you become."

— GISELE BUNDCHEN

CHAPTER 23

"All our dreams can come true if we have the COURAGE to pursue them."

— WALT DISNEY

Having purpose can give you the passion that you are looking for. When you want something bad enough, the Universe will respond. You must only open your arms and your heart to receive it. Do not allow anything to distract you from what you want. Do not let anyone tell you that you cannot do it. Be daring. Be yourself. Be ready to change. Be ready to find your purpose.

Sometimes the only way to deal with naysayers is to rebel. Rebel against the negativity. Rebel against your comfort zone. Focus on your desires. Focus on your purpose. Do not allow anyone's negativity to distract you from your desires and your purpose. You deserve to have what you want. Never stop believing in yourself.

No matter what happens, you must never stop believing that you can do it. There are so many possibilities in life. You were born to be great. You have everything within you to find your potential. Your potential is endless.

Never ignore your own potential; be obsessed with it. Yes, it takes courage to live the life you desire, but it's worth it. Do not let negative self-talk hold you back from what you desire. Stop setting limits on your life. You can do whatever the hell you want to do!

Zig Ziglar said, "When you catch a glimpse of your potential, that's when passion is born."

Your dreams are all there, in your heart. You must learn to unleash them and recognize that your dreams are important. You must recognize your potential. You must give yourself permission to go after your dreams, and you will find your passion.

I have been asked many times, "How do I find my passion?" I always answer with this: look back to your childhood and remember what made you happy; remember what you dreamed you wanted to do when you grew up. Look into your heart and think about what you would do if you were not afraid to do it. You will find the answer you seek if you look deep enough. Fear kills dreams faster than anything. Allow your inner instincts to lead you for a change. Do not be afraid of failure, because what if you don't fail? What if you succeed? Stop the self-doubt and go in the direction of your childhood dreams. Have the courage to listen to your heart. You have nothing to lose, and so much to gain.

"A lot of people never use their initiative because no one told them to."

— BANSKY

Initiative is the ability to solve problems and take action without being told to do so.

It's important for us to realize that we cannot wait around for someone else to do what we want done. There is no perfect moment to accomplish what you desire. There is only now.

Initiative is about being proactive and being responsible to ourselves. Each one of us has the ability to choose. Each one of us has the ability to make anything that we desire happen for us. Success will only come to those who choose to take action.

If I did not take the initiative to begin writing my book, it would never have gotten done. If I did not take the initiative to sit down at the computer every day, my book would never have been published. If I did not take the initiative to approach Best Sellers Publishing Academy, my book would not be in the hands of all my special readers today.

There is no perfect moment to accomplish what you desire. There is only now. Now is the time to be doing what you love, and what you want to do.

We each have the ability within us to choose. It's about being proactive and being responsible for our own lives.

Persistence is the key. Action is the lock. Put the key to persistence into the lock of action, and open the door to change.

Nothing will happen for us if we cannot make the decision to change the situation.

The most basic of human needs is to find your purpose. We cannot go through life without a passion for something. Something that makes your heart race. Something that lights up your life. Something that gives us complete satisfaction. Something that makes us excited to awaken every morning. Something that gets us worked up and ready to live each new day.

I actually say aloud to myself every morning, after I've had my 2 or 3 cups of coffee: "It's time to get my party started."

Make each day a party.

If it is needed, make a radical change in yourself. Do not be afraid to take it to the next level. Cut the toxic people out of your life. Make the first move toward a better you. Too many people live in unhappy relationships. Too many people live in fear of change. Too many people live with an unhappy situation because they are conditioned to that life. I must tell you that the joys in life come from new experiences. Be bold, be brave; do the things you have not previously done. Do not be defined by your present situation. Amazing things happen when you let go of your limiting beliefs and learn to go for it. Make each day something to look forward to!

You already have what it takes. You just need to let it loose! Take responsibility for your actions. Have some gumption and just go for it! We will find the change that we are looking for if we search deep within our hearts, and just begin.

Stop wishing and start doing!

"It's only after you've stepped outside your comfort zone that you begin to change, grow, and transform."

— ROY T. BENNET

CHAPTER 24

"If the path that you are on isn't taking you where you want to go, then choose a different path."

— LINDA BREEDLOVE

No one ever told us that life will be easy. No one told us that we would have all the answers. Life will become more difficult and more complicated. Choosing the right path in life will not be easy.

How do I know that this is the right path? How do I know I want to go in this direction? Is this the right direction for me? It comes down to trusting in your own instincts. It comes down to trusting the feelings in your gut. Your intuition will tell you if you are on the right path. If you are not getting a good feeling about this particular path, then change direction. You are not stuck in one spot; you have feet and they can move you in whatever direction you choose.

Often the people around us—family, spouses, and friends—will try to push us in directions that they like, and feel would be good for us. Please always follow your own instincts. You must only go where you feel right. You must find your own path. Do not be bullied into going in a direction that you do not feel comfortable in. The most difficult path is the one that you take alone, but that is where you must go to find your true self.

Always remember to follow your own path. Obstacles are put in your way to test you, and to help you understand that what you are doing and desiring to do is really worth fighting for. Your path will be your path and your path alone. You will be exactly where you want to be when you decide that your path is the one you want to follow. Always remember that you can change direction if you find your path is not taking you to the place you want.

Each path will be different, and we must be willing to choose the right direction that is important to each one of us. Do not try to follow someone else's path, for it will not lead you to where you want to go. Your own path will take you in the direction of your own dreams. I cannot tell you enough to remember there are thousands of directions that you can go, and if the path you are on isn't leading to where you want to be, then change paths! Be strong and take the path less traveled. Above all, trust your own gut instincts, and always be true to yourself.

The path that I follow is different from the path you may follow. That simply means that we have different dreams and goals. It means I have different passions. It means I have a different purpose.

I just want you to know that you are strong, and you can follow your path.

Find your own purpose, and your path will lead you to the place you wish to be.

"What sets you apart can sometimes feel like a burden and it's not. And a lot of the time, it's what makes you great."

— EMMA STONE

CHAPTER 25

> "Feelings are those little things that keep dancing in your heart and your mind and are often difficult to let go."
>
> — LINDA BREEDLOVE

Feelings are just exactly that—feelings. Yes, we are entitled to our feelings. Yes, our feelings are important.

Sensitive people have deeper feelings and appreciate the simpler things in life. We feel things more. We love deeper, and we are loyal and true to the important people in our lives, and to ourselves. We tend to be old fashioned in our thinking and tend to be more philosophical about our existence. We are more creative and dream more. We also open ourselves up to be hurt more.

I tend to let my feelings be known a lot. I have always been an "upfront kind of person." My feelings are always very apparent in my face; always have been. It's not something that I do on purpose. It's not something that I am able to hide very effectively. I would much rather be able to hide my feelings sometimes because I often get told I am too emotional, or I should not let my feelings be so apparent. Where I do get into trouble is when I let my feelings control my actions. Having feelings and being sensitive is not a bad thing; we simply need to learn how to control those feelings. It does not make you a weak person to have feelings. I feel it makes you stronger.

Let me tell you this: our feelings are valid. Letting our feelings control us is not what we want, though. We do not have to control our feelings, but we do need to control our actions with them. This is not easy to do if you act with your heart, as I do.

Some people are not good at expressing and explaining their feelings; some are too vocal with them. Being alone with your feelings is not an easy place to be. Sometimes you must release those feelings to be able to clear your mind and go on.

I remember my mother telling me to keep my feelings to myself, unless I was asked about them. Her other words of wisdom at that same time were to never, ever take things personally. "What others say and do is their own, not yours to worry about."

"In the process of letting go you will lose many things from the past,
but you will find yourself."

— DEEPAK CHOPRA

I have been having some feelings of guilt lately. I dislike feeling guilty for anything. I keep telling myself what is done is done; there is no point at all rehashing it repeatedly in your mind. Reliving the mistake over and over will only ruin your happiness of today.

What did I do wrong? What is the reason for my guilt? Could I have done something else to make it better? These are all questions that run through my mind when I think about the impossible situation that has presented itself to me.

Guilt is one of the most useless emotions we can have; it's right up there with worry. Never play the victim roles. Love who you are and take responsibility for your own actions. It is okay to be wrong sometimes, and it is okay to take care of yourself first. Everyone is entitled to make mistakes. That is where your learning comes from. Your mistakes do not make you a bad person. Making mistakes is all part of being human. When you accept your guilt, you will be able to release it. While we cannot undo something from the past, we can leave it in the past where it belongs and go on from there.

Do not let anyone push you into feeling guilty. They are manipulating you into feelings of self-doubt and a submissive position. When another person stirs up the guilt trip, they are trying to justify their own unacceptable behaviour. We are not responsible for what others feel.

It is time to live in the present and stop the guilt right in its tracks. Do not let the past hold you hostage anymore. You are not the same person you were before. No amount of guilt is going to change what happened before. Do not be so hard on yourself. Your thoughts are important to your wellbeing, so change them. Let it all go.

Live in the present, and you will be much happier.

> "Between stimulus and response there is a space. In that space is our power to choose our response. In our response lies our growth and our freedom."
>
> — VIKTOR E. FRANKL

CHAPTER 26

> "The ocean's tides are a result of gravitational forces. The ocean cannot resist those forces. Be like the ocean, and do not resist the changes that come our way."
>
> — LINDA BREEDLOVE

There is nothing more beautiful and calming than the ocean. When you need something to diminish your stress, look to the ocean. It inspires your mind and helps the creativity flow.

I grew up with the ocean at my front door, and the beach as my playground. I have never left it for exceptionally long periods of time. It draws me close with its beauty and brings much joy to my heart.

The continual movement of the waves and the tide is a gentle reminder that everything changes with time and whatever direction you flow.

One of the greatest lessons that I learned on my journey, was that life does not always go as planned. Sometimes you end up going in another direction all together. Life will always have twists and turns and bumps in the road. All we can do is control the pace in which things happen. We cannot directly control the changes that happen.

The ocean's tides are constantly changing; they ebb, and they flow. They can be furious, or they can be gentle and calm, but the tides' movements are constant; each change is as beautiful as the next.

Just as we cannot stop the tides from changing, we cannot stop the changes that cross our paths. These are the changes that happen when you least expect them. They often come at you with a thud! They often require you to look beneath the surface to see what is happening underneath, just as you can look beneath the surface of the ocean's tides and watch the sand and pebbles move with the direction of the flow.

These changes that you encounter can enter your life at a time just when you think you have everything all mapped out. Just when you think your life is where you want it to be, something happens to change it.

You cannot stop the waves from happening. You cannot stop the ebb and the flow of the tide. Change is inevitable. You can learn to go with the flow though.

You will end up exactly where you are meant to be, just as the tide ends up exactly where it is meant to be.

Nothing stays the same. We cannot stop the tides. We cannot stop change. We must learn to go with the flow just as the tide. Be loyal to your change. Be loyal to your own future. Be loyal to yourself.

The decision is yours to make, and yours alone when you are faced with changes.

Embrace the changes.

The ocean embraces change every day.

"Lovely thing to learn from water: adjust yourself in every situation, and in any shape. But most importantly, find your own way to flow."

— BUDDHA'S TEACHING AND SCIENCE

I tend to have strong beliefs and principles. I am learning to have some flexibility with myself though. I am learning that not everything has to be set in stone.

Allowing change is necessary for my own peace of mind. Allowing myself to adapt to a situation, any situation is tantamount to my own psychological health.

As we navigate through this journey called life, we all have beliefs and values that are important to us. Some of our values and beliefs come straight from our childhood. Some we acquire through our experiences during our lifetime.

Most of us understand that our belief system has shaped us into the person we are.

Throughout my journey discovering my purpose, I've learned that a strong belief system is vital to my existence. I am grateful for everything that has happened to me in the past or I would not have these principles and beliefs that have made me into the person I am today.

I have been known to be stubborn about my goals and dreams, but I had to learn to be flexible in my approach to reach those goals. Not everything that we do or believe in must consume our very existence. We can learn to adapt to situations, and we can learn to bend our own rules if necessary.

We all need to feel secure in our beliefs. However, we all need to understand and be secure that we will attain our goals even if we may have to change some of our own personal approaches. Change is the necessary part of finding our passions. If we are not willing to bend our own sense of rules, we will end up breaking them. I feel that the more secure I am about attaining my goals, the more it feels like it's not the end of the world if I must bend my own rules. Our power is in our ability to be flexible.

I am stubborn about my goals; however, I am working hard on being flexible about attaining them.

CANADA POST POSTES CANADA
Mail Courrier
BE Kind
BE Calm
BE
THANK You Postal Workers
Canada

CHAPTER 27

> "Learn the alchemy true human beings know.
> The moment you accept what troubles you've
> been given; the door will open."
>
> — RUMI

Learning acceptance. This is what filled my thoughts at 4:00 AM. Learning to accept myself and change what I cannot accept in myself.

Acceptance does not mean forgiveness. However, forgiveness will free your heart from sadness if you choose that.

Nothing ever stays the same, and as soon as we learn that, we will gain the power to change our lives. We can then look back with the realization that we are responsible for ourselves. We are responsible for our own energies. We are responsible for our own peace and contentment.

Do not focus on what you are giving up when you do change; only focus on what you will gain from this change.

We must understand ourselves and accept the person that we are while continuing to work towards the changes we desire to see in ourselves.

Acceptance is the key to self-realization. Life is not about being perfect, life is about trusting in the journey and accepting who we are in order to move on to something that we truly desire in our lives.

Acceptance means growth. Acceptance means figuring out who we really are. It means being responsive to change and building something new. We can only change ourselves; we cannot change anyone else around us. Life is full of uncertainties. There is no point in worrying about the uncertainties. Accept those uncertainties and change only what you are certain of: you, and only you.

Changing yourself will open the door to new opportunities. It does not matter if you failed in the past; it only matters how you react to it. Progress will never happen to those that are not willing to change.

If it's not in your control, do not let it consume your life.

Buddha very wisely said, "There are three solutions to every problem: accept it, change it, or leave it. If you cannot accept it, change it. If you cannot change it, leave it."

There is a song that was sung by Andy Williams many years ago, "Dream the Impossible Dream."

My mother used to sing this song along with Andy Williams on the record player. There is a verse in that song that resonates with me still, even after all these years.

"This is my quest, to follow that star

No matter how hopeless, no matter how far to fight for the right

Without question or pause

To be willing to march

Into hell for a heavenly cause."

You must fight for what you believe in. No matter how hopeless it may seem at the time.

> "You don't become what you want,
> you become what you believe."
>
> — OPRAH WINFREY

You must believe in yourself. You must have faith that you will become what it is that you want to become.

Never give up on your dreams. If you can desire your dream enough, you can make it happen. Your dream is achievable when you believe with all your heart and soul that it can happen. You must believe with all your heart that you deserve what you are desiring to do. Never forget that you are capable of whatever you choose to be.

Be positive in your approach. Be disciplined in your actions to attain your dreams. Celebrate the fact that you can and will do anything you put your mind to. Never double your abilities, and NEVER ignore your own potential.

Your dreams and desires are important; never give up on something you truly wish to do. Your dreams matter. Your desires are important. Trust your instincts, and just go for it. You can literally create the life you have imagined if you have a firm belief that you can do it, and if you are willing to do the work required to attain that dream. You must be willing to do the work, though! Desires and dreams are the beginning. You must then be active in your approach to attain those dreams. Action is the necessary part of attaining that dream.

Believing in yourself takes just as much energy as doubting yourself. Which one would you choose? I know I choose to believe in myself over doubting myself. You have the power in your mind to change doubt to belief.

You will be amazed at what you attract when you believe in your own self. Master that belief, and no one can take it away from you. Everything in your life will begin to change when you work hard at what you believe in. The only limits you have are in your own mind. Get rid of the doubt and believe that you can do what you wish to do.

Your destiny is yours to control. If the opportunity does not come knocking, you can create your own opportunity.

Dream the Impossible Dream.

> "Everyone thinks about changing the world,
> no one thinks about changing himself."
>
> — LEO TOLSTOY

CHAPTER 28

"Life is a journey that's measured not in miles or years, but in experiences."

— JIMMY BUFFET

Life is full of adventure. It is always a gamble and risk. Nothing stays the same forever.

Keep that in mind and you will always have adventures. Live the life you dream about and you will always have adventures. Make the most out of your life and make each day an adventure. The mountain is there waiting for you, but the adventure is in the climb.

Everyone's journey will be different from yours.

We will have some great instances in our lives, and we will have some not so great occurrences. We will be faced with extraordinary and not so extraordinary people. However, everyone we meet will have some sort of impact on each and every one of us. That impact may be memorable immediately, or it may come to you later in small doses, a little at a time.

You never know what kind of impact you will have on those you encounter. Every interaction that we have will impact others. Make those interactions positive and leave a little of yourself with them. People will remember you for how you made them feel. Leave everyone feeling good.

Through it all, it will be the relationships that we form throughout our journey that will shape our lives. Whether these relationships are good ones or not so good, they will be a part of us forever.

Life is a privilege. What we send out will come back to us. Always send out good vibes to be on the receiving end of those good vibes. Always look for the good in people. Do not judge, and above all, appreciate the differences that we all have. No two people are exactly the same. We all have different goals and dreams. We all have different aspirations. We all embark on our life's journey with different outlooks and purposes.

Sometimes we will be faced with some unquestionably difficult lessons. These are meant to make us into a better human being. Our struggles are simply a way for us to learn. Our intuition will help lead the way for us. Always listen to your instincts. They will show you the way.

I have learned throughout my lifetime that my heart leads the way for me, and my gut instinct tells me if it is the right thing to do. If I happen to make a mistake, it is just a lesson to be learned from. I will try hard to not make the same mistake twice. My mission in life is to enjoy it with all the gusto that I can possibly have. My experiences have made me into the person that I am today. It did not matter if some of those experiences were good or bad; I am who I am because of them.

Embrace the unknown. Embrace the uncertainty. Be brave and travel the least known path.

Go beyond the usual, and live this adventure called life. Make it an epic one.

"Goodbyes are only for those who love with their eyes. Because for those who love with heart and soul there is no such thing as separation."

— RUMI

CHAPTER 29

"Secrecy is the enemy of intimacy. Every healthy relationship is built on a foundation of trust."

— DAVEWILLIS.ORG

Did you know that even elephants know how to trust each other and be trustworthy? It is a proven fact that empathy and trust are key characteristics of an elephant herd. Their empathetic behaviour is the way they communicate with each other and the trust allows the strong bonds between the herd. They seem to know and understand instinctively that they must trust in each other for the safety of their entire herd.

Trust is built. Trust is earned. Love might be unconditional, but trusting one another in a relationship, any kind of relationship, is not unconditional. Trust is the most important aspect in a relationship. Without trust, you will never make it to the end with each other.

Honesty and trust in any relationship is by far the most important.

Even one lie can create doubt. When you find out you have been lied to for years, any trust and respect you had is gone.

If you cannot trust the other person, you do not have a relationship; you have a convenience.

You cannot love someone you do not trust. You begin to question everything that they have told you in the past. You begin to question whether they truly did love you. Trust, respect, and love go together.

It takes years to build trust and mere moments to lose it. Even one lie told is enough to create doubt in any future you may have together.

You cannot build trust back quickly. Even if it is somehow repairable, there will always be some doubt in every action and every word. There will always be some uncertainty. There will always be something that will be broken. You can say sorry a thousand times, and you can say "I love you" over and over, but if you do not have trust in that person, those words mean absolutely nothing. If you cannot show that you are sorry by changing your behaviour, your words will have no meaning at all.

When you have given so much of yourself to the other person, it is a difficult lesson to learn. It hurts when you find out that you were not important enough to them, for them to tell you the truth. You begin to wonder if they have ever been completely honest with you. Even one lie can make you question all of what you have been told by that person.

When you finally realize that you have been lied to and manipulated for a long time, you feel disillusioned and somehow responsible. You begin to get incredibly sad first, and then angry with yourself, for allowing them to be untruthful with you. You get angry with yourself because you ignored the warning signals for years. Then you get angry with yourself for not coming to terms with it earlier. You even ignored the little snippets of doubt that have a habit of creeping into your mind. You give the other person the benefit of that doubt even though in your heart you felt something was not right. Things did not add up. You even begin to think you are just being paranoid. Then, like a ton of bricks, it hits you, and hits hard! No one should ever be treated with such disrespect. Then you realize you have been deceived. Deceit is not only manipulative; it is heart-shattering.

Even when the other person offers you an apology, you can accept the apology, but you will still have great difficulty in trusting them again. **Apologies are for mistakes made, and lying to you is not a mistake.**

Lying to you is a decision. An apology from someone without them changing their behaviour is a form of manipulation.

Being in a relationship does not guarantee that the relationship will last forever. It takes respect, trust, understanding, and love. Without those, no relationship will last. Any relationship is doomed without trust. Without trust there is no reason to continue.

You can forgive the person, but the difficulty lies in the inability to trust them again fully. There will always be that little bit of doubt. The best proof of someone absolutely loving you is in their ability to maintain that modicum of trust and not using that trust against you. When someone truly loves you, they will not lie to you. It is only cowards that will hide behind the truth. When someone lies to you, it's because they do not respect you enough to be honest. The worst feeling in the world is when someone you have trusted lies to you. Lies and love cannot coexist.

Apologies without change mean nothing.

> "The world exists as you perceive it.
> It is not what you see... but how you see it.
> It is not what you hear...but how you hear it.
> It is not what you feel...but how you feel it."
>
> — RUMI

Would you like to join my pity party? When people feel sorry for themselves, it's usually because they are not happy with their present situation.

I was feeling sorry for myself, believing that it was extenuating circumstances that put me in that current situation.

In reality, it was me that put myself in that situation. I had to reach deep inside myself to understand that. Sometimes these situations happen simply to teach you a valuable lesson. They teach you to be grateful. Grateful for what you do have. Gratitude is the key to happiness.

Focussing on the negative will only make it worse. Do not wait for someone else to 'make it better.' You and you alone are the only one that can make it better for yourself. You are the captain of your own ship. Search for the good in the unpleasant situation and realize that you and only you can make it better. No one owes you anything. Your life is what you make of it. You must help yourself.

Feeling sorry for yourself is only a complete waste of time and energy. Never allow someone else's negative behaviour to affect yours. That is giving them power over you and you will have lost your self worth.

If you mope around feeling sorry for yourself, good things will not happen for you. Life does not work like that. You must send out positive vibes for the positive vibes to come back to you.

You are in charge of your own life, do not assign that power to anyone else, EVER! Self-pity is a complete waste of your time and energy. Instead focus on what you and you alone can do about it to make it better. It's time to cancel your pity party. Pull yourself together, take charge and own your life.

Take responsibility, get up, get moving and do something about your present situation.

We can continue to focus on what is bad in our lives or we can focus on what is good. The choice belongs to us and only us.

“A woman with a voice is,
by definition, a strong woman.”

— MELINDA GATES

CHAPTER 30

"Change is inevitable,
but transformation is by conscious choice."

— HEATHER ASH AMARA

I did not wake up one day and decide to transform myself. It came to me in smaller "Aha!" moments.

I changed my lifestyle. I changed my eating habits. I spent many moments agonizing on how I was going to make these positive changes and keep them. I began to realize that, for these changes to become permanent for me, I had to begin slowly at first. I told myself that no matter what my present circumstances were, they did not determine my outcome. I had told myself that everything I was going through was merely the beginning of my transformation. I still had many miles to go on this journey. I told myself that I am what I *do,* not what I say I am *going* to do.

I looked at myself as a project. I desired the transformation so strongly that I gave myself no other option except to change. This requires time, commitment, and a copious amount of courage.

You first must learn to love yourself unconditionally. Stop apologizing for being you. Celebrate the unstoppable and beautiful you. What you decide to change is up to you, and only up to you. Do it for yourself, and only for yourself. If you are brave enough to make changes with your life, you will be unstoppable. It's not about being perfect; it's about the inner desires that you wish to see in yourself. Making a huge transformation in your life is scary, but if you do not make the change that you desire to make, you will have regrets. Regrets are scarier.

I recently made a huge transformation in my life.

I had a mommy makeover.

I had plastic surgery. I had, in medical terms, abdominoplasty and a mastopexy. I had lived with loose tummy skin and droopy breasts for years, (compliments of birthing babies and weight loss) and instead of complaining about it, I finally made the decision to do something about it.

Having these procedures is not for the faint of heart. I was warned about the pain and discomfort, and I thought I was prepared…

You will need to summon up all the courage that you have in your heart and soul. Tummy tucks and breast lifts are not simple procedures. There is a lot of pain the first few days after the surgery. My tummy felt like it had been run over by a truck—the muscles hurt every time I moved. Coughing is painful. Even sneezing hurts your breasts! I had to sleep in a reclining position for many weeks. Walking with your back straight was impossible for the first few days. The trauma that your body goes through is ten times worse than what I expected. Even though I was warned, I was determined to go through with this transformation.

I was admitted to the hospital early in the morning on a Friday. The surgery was scheduled for around 8:00 am. I was feeling a little unnerved sitting and waiting for it to happen. My surgeon was coming to see me before the procedure, so I was waiting patiently in my hospital gown in my little cubicle. The feeling of fear kept creeping into my mind. *Am I crazy? Why am I putting myself through this?* Then my doctor came into the room and said he needed to draw where the nipples were going to be placed on my breasts and where the breasts were going to be.

Gulp!

He then proceeded to put marks on my breasts with a black pen so he would know where to cut and place the nipples. It was quite comical, having breasts drawn on your breasts.

I was then walked into surgery, laid on the surgical table, and anesthetized.

My breasts were cut around the underside and a cut right up to the nipple. The nipples were also removed and repositioned. The excess skin was removed. The breast was then filled with the tissue that was already there and raised. The nipples were placed, and the breasts were firm again.

My tummy was cut from hip to hip. The tummy was suctioned of any extra fat, and the loose skin removed. The belly button was removed and repositioned in the center of the abdomen. The surgery took almost four hours to complete. The insides were stitched with dissolvable stitches, and the outside was covered in suture tapes. So, if you are contemplating this type of surgery, you will want to think long and hard first, because it is a major operation.

The pain lasted for about eight days, which is not too long. However, the itching took much longer to go away. The itching is intense. It itches around the nipples and around the suture tapes. It itches on the suture tapes on the abdomen. Pain is one thing, but itching is worse. You cannot scratch because the areas are too sensitive. It took weeks for the itching to subside. Vitamin E oil helps considerably, but you cannot apply it until all the surgical suture tapes have fallen off.

There will also be scars. There are always scars after this type of surgery—deep, raw, red scars across the lower abdomen, and underneath the breast. These scars will fade with time, but they will be with you for the rest of your life.

During the recovery period, you are required to wear a heavy compression garment that wraps around your abdomen, and it is the most uncomfortable body piece I have ever had to wear. A special fitting bra is also necessary when you have the mastopexy.

The bra is not too uncomfortable; however, it's not terribly pretty. I could not wait to get it off and begin wearing pretty and lacy undergarments again.

The full recovery process takes about six weeks. So, you must be absolutely positive that you want these procedures done, because there is a lot of pain and discomfort post-surgery.

Even though I was content enough with my body image before the surgery, I had wanted both procedures for several years. I could not let it go from my mind. I made the decision to go for it after deciding that, if I wanted it desperately enough, I should do it. **I did it for me, and only me**. It's not that I wanted to have a perfect body; I simply wanted my body to reflect what I felt in my heart.

We can take a lesson from the caterpillar. The caterpillar undergoes massive changes to become the beautiful butterfly. It does not happen overnight though; it takes time for the caterpillar to build her cocoon for her transformation into the beautiful butterfly to be complete.

The best thing I ever did for me was believe in myself. I changed my mindset, my body, and my life!

Please do not for one moment think that I am advocating these surgical procedures, because they are painful and take a long time to recover from. I made these bold decisions for myself, and only for myself. Growing and changing is never easy, but when you truly desire those changes, you must do it. It will all be worth it the end.

I am completely happy with my decision and my body. I do not regret a moment the pain or the discomfort that I had to bear.

If you make the decision to have these procedures done, please make sure you go to a respected and reputable surgeon. My surgeon is exceedingly well respected, and well known in his field of expertise.

"No one ever became a success without taking chances... One must be able to recognize the moment and seize it without delay."

— ESTÉE LAUDER

CHAPTER 31

"Doubt kills more dreams than failure ever will."

— KARIM SEDDIKI

Do you ever doubt yourself? Do you ever doubt your choices? Do you doubt your feelings?

Doubting ourselves comes from too much thinking, and not enough doing.

Sometimes we must tell our mind to "just shut up!" Doubt kills dreams and desires. Never doubt yourself.

Everything will work out exactly as it is supposed to. Doubt is the enemy of growth. It is the enemy of change. Doubting yourself uses the same amount of energy that believing in yourself does. Instead of searching within yourself for reasons why something will not work, look deeper to find the reasons why it will.

When you find you are doubting yourself, look for as many positives as you can find, and release all the negatives.

Doubt is being insecure about yourself. Remember, you are infinitely capable of doing whatever it is your heart desires. Have faith in your journey. Make your faith in yourself stronger than your fears. Never compare your progress to anyone else's. Your dreams and desires are yours, and yours alone. Be consistent. You will only fail if you stop trying. Be the best version of yourself. If someone tells you that you cannot do something, PROVE THEM WRONG.

If your concern is that someone may not like what you are doing, do not give it a second thought. It does not matter what you do; there will always be someone who will talk about you. They may question your choices. They may judge you. They may even be offended by your actions. Remember this. Remember that whatever anyone else thinks about you is a reflection of their own selves. It has nothing, I repeat, nothing to do with you. Someone will always judge you and dislike you, or your actions.

Do not take anything they may say or do personally. It has nothing to do with you, and everything to do with them.

Just be yourself. Make your own choices and decisions for yourself, not for anyone else's opinions of you.

You cannot please everyone, so do not even bother trying. At the end of the day, it's your own self that you have made happy, not anyone else.

Love yourself unconditionally. Believe in yourself. Find your own inner peace.

There is where your power lies.

We all have it in our power to change our attitudes and our lives if we truly desire the changes. Become so damn confident in yourself that you have no other choice but to finish what you have started. Do not let anyone's opinion or anyone else's doubt and misgivings stop you from doing what you have dreamed of doing. Embrace your inner warrior. Feel the power from completing your goals. Make a heartfelt promise to yourself that you will keep going forward. Whatever has been holding you back, just let it go and begin. You can move slowly but just keep moving. Hang in there, growth and experiences come with time.

CHAPTER 32

Are You Ready to Shift into High Gear?

Are you ready to make the changes you have been wanting to make?

Are you ready to make changes in your ability to motivate yourself to make decisions?

Changing yourself is not an easy task. Discovering things about yourself that you do not like is difficult.

I have been asked many times, "Did you just wake up one day and decide that you wanted to change yourself? How do you make changes in yourself? How do you keep those changes?"

The answer to the first question is, yes. I did just wake up one day and make the decision to change. I did not know how at that time, but I knew that I had to for my own health, self-esteem, and peace of mind.

I was not happy with what and who I had become. I had lost myself somewhere in between becoming a mother, and my children leaving home.

I actually made the decision to change one morning at 4:00 AM, and I consciously made the decision to act on that desire right then and there. I decided that I was going to do everything in my power to be the person that I desired to be.

The transformation did not happen all at once, or right away. I knew it would take me a lot of time to get to those changes that I desired.

I first had to search deep within to find what I wanted to change. I had to be truly honest and critical with everything that I was not happy with. This exercise is probably the most difficult because who wants to know all our own faults and misgivings. But being completely honest with yourself is necessary before you will be able to continue with the changes that you desire.

You finally figure out that you cannot change all things and you do not have to. You realize that you cannot change the people around you—you can only change yourself, your attitude, and your reactions.

You figure out that learning to love yourself again is the first and most important step. You realize that there are things within yourself that you really do love. When you realize this, you will discover that there are things that you can change, and that you deserve to change them to become the person you wish to become. Just remember that any changes you make must be with yourself and only yourself.

The changes you wish to make to yourself must become almost an obsession, because all of us do become comfortable with who we are and resist the urge to make changes.

First you must list the changes that you desire. Seeing them in print makes them become real.

You get to decide what changes you want to make. You can set goals for becoming happier. You can set goals to become healthier. You can set goals to become more confident. It's all up to you.

Just make the decision and put action behind that decision.

Recording those goals is important because you will be able to see what changes you desire each day and remind yourself why you want to make these changes. Make your goals as ambitious as you want. Work hard every single day to attain them. Wake up each morning, read your goals over and over, and then read them again.

Be ready to "kick ass" every day.

Do not fall prey to the "I can't syndrome." Focus on the reasons for the changes you want. Continue repeating each morning the reasons why you desire these changes. Remind yourself that you have the ability and the capabilities to affect whatever change you desire in yourself. Set those goals, and slam them!

You will only get back what you put into your desires. Strive each day for progress; even a little progress each day is better than none. Be determined. Become obsessed with those changes. Become obsessed with the person that you desire to be.

Studies have shown that it is common for women as they age to lose self-esteem and confidence in themselves. It is common for us to dislike our body image as we age. Remember that you have always been beautiful and intelligent; you just somehow lost a little bit of yourself over the years. It's time now to regain that and take control of your life again.

It's time to become happier, and healthier. It is time to become more confident in yourself. It is time to feel like you can conquer anything in your way again. Obstacles become steppingstones when you are more confident in yourself.

There are many procedures and resources available to us nowadays to help us to feel more confident in ourselves again, and to raise our self-esteem again. There are so many non-invasive procedures that will help to keep your skin young, healthy and fresh looking.

Keeping our bodies active is important to our wellbeing. Remember to also keep your mind active.

The decision is yours to make. You are one decision away from a better and happier you. Remember, your fresh start is waiting for you. You just need to desire those changes bad enough that you are willing to work hard to attain them.

You will encounter some difficulties along the way. No one said it would be easy, but it will be worth every bit of the process.

Remember though, your desired outcome will happen for you only if you are willing to put in the work to attain it.

CHAPTER 33

Conclusion:

Life is so short. Most of us spend way too much time worrying about things—things that have a 99% chance of NOT happening. We all tend to "sweat the small stuff."

We complain; we compare ourselves to others; we always want something better or bigger than our neighbors, and we cannot seem to just be happy and content with what we have.

Please remember, it is not wrong to want more. It is not wrong to want to make improvements to ourselves. We simply need to put into perspective what the reasons are for wanting more. If you truly desire those changes, then go for it, but if you want those changes for the wrong reasons (like only wanting to be better than your neighbour) then you must refocus on the simpler things, and be happy with what you have. You must decide for yourself the reasons for desiring the changes, and those reasons must be for you and you only.

Focus on being grateful for what you do have and stop complaining about what you do not have. Instead, work towards being a better person, and get clear on what you really, truly want from your life.

You will realize that what you truly desire are not "things," but accomplishments and experiences.

There have been many times in my life when I thought I wanted more material things. I was confused about what I really needed. And honestly, I had no clue that what I really wanted was to find my purpose. I needed to find my passion. Living my life on purpose and having a passion gave me the happiness and contentment that I was searching for.

Today, though I know what I want—and I am doing what I want—I am still looking to find more. Not material things, though. I want to do more, I want to experience more, I want to live more! There is so much more to discover during this journey called life, and I am not stopping in my quest now.

I have a clear vision of what I want from my life now. I have discovered that I want to help other women and men be the best that they can be. I have learned to listen to my heart, for it knows the way to a fulfilling life for me.

With that being said, there are still times where I kick myself in the butt to keep myself going ahead. I often must redirect my thoughts to keep going when things become challenging and difficult. I have learned that a good kick in the backside is all I need to refocus and harness the power of my mind.

Theodore Roosevelt said, "If you could kick the person in the pants responsible for most of your trouble, you wouldn't sit for a month."

I have tried many things during my adulthood to find my true passion. I think most of us do, and that is okay—keep searching for the right things to fill your life. Just take the time to write these things in your journal that you wish to discover, and the places that you wish to go. These are your dreams, and your goals. Cross them off your list when you have accomplished them. If they did not give you the satisfaction that you were looking for, then add more to your list. You are not stuck with your original plans; you have the right to change them anytime you wish. They are, after all your dreams and desires.

I had to go back to my childhood to remember what I truly loved to do. When I finally remembered, I followed the path that I began as a ten-year-old and had forgotten all about when I became an adult.

Each day reminds us that everything changes; nothing stays the same. Each day brings us a new beginning. That new beginning is our reminder that we can change as well. It's not about perfection.

It's about how hard we can work towards the changes we desire. Perfection is not the goal. It is about your own personal growth.

Change your thoughts and change your beliefs.

It is a proven fact that we can rewire our brains with our thoughts and our emotions. We can train our brain to react and function differently. As soon as we make the conscious decision to change, our brain will act accordingly. However, we must keep telling our brain that we desire this change. Our brains are constantly accepting new things through our daily experiences. I have learned that we can control how we think, and how we act.

There is a term for this: neuroplasticity, which refers to our brain's ability to reorganize our thoughts in all situations, including environment, behaviour emotions, and thoughts.

Whatever circumstances we grew up with, or whatever happened in our childhood can be changed, improved, and made stronger by changing our beliefs. We need to embrace many different experiences and keep our brains active with learning, reading, and discovering new things. We need to make ourselves uncomfortable at times and change our current thoughts and mindset. By changing just a few simple beliefs and actions, we can alter our brain's neurochemistry.

Our brain will do what we tell it to do. Tell it to do good and tell it to be positive. Tell it to love unconditionally. Tell it that change is a necessary part of growth. We exist in a world of amazing opportunities. At any point in our lives, we can change direction.

Today is full of new possibilities. We are worthy of our dreams and goals. Change your internal belief system to believe that you can, and you will achieve your dreams and goals.

Believe simply means to accept something as true. To have faith, confidence, and trust.

Believe that you will fulfill your dreams and goals, and you will. Believe everything will work out in the end and it will. Believe that your life is amazing, and it is. Believe that you will succeed, and you will.

"The scariest thing about distance is you don't know whether they'll miss you, or forget about you."

— NICHOLAS SPARKS, *The Notebook.*

Does distance really make the heart grow fonder? Or does it just seem that way because you yearn for that person?

Does it make you feel sad or even angry that you cannot be with that person? Or does it make you happy to think that they have you in their heart, and you have them in yours, so that is enough? Can you be grateful for the times that you do spend together?

Is the bond you share strong enough to survive thousands of miles? Is that bond enough?

Good relationships are worth fighting for. Working hard at maintaining what you have is necessary if you want to keep the relationship. Do not give up too easily.

Distance between two lovers is never an easy situation. True love is worth the wait though. Cherish the times that you do have together.

I believe that distance creates an emptiness that cannot be filled until you are with that person again. It creates a special bond that makes you feel invincible. It makes you realize that love comes in many different ways. Perhaps distance gives you a reason to love harder? Perhaps distance makes us see things clearer? Perhaps distance helps us realize exactly just how much that person means to us?

The truth is, distance never really separates people that really care for each other. Sometimes circumstances will separate you from the people you love the most, but that does not mean you love them any less. If two hearts can survive distance and time apart, they are truly in love, and they can overcome any obstacles. When you love someone with all your heart, and that love is reciprocated, you are connected with your souls.

Missing someone is a natural part of loving someone. Missing that person reminds your heart that you love them. You cannot break the bond of someone that you absolutely love with distance. I feel that being apart from someone that you genuinely love makes you realize just how much you do love that person. If that love is strong, you will find ways to overcome the challenges that you are facing by being thousands of miles apart. If the relationship matters, the distance will not.

It is of no importance where you are because you are, under the same sky. You are under the same stars, and the same moon. Distance cannot stop what is meant to be. Distance cannot stop you from loving someone.

Whether your love is 3 miles away or 3,000 miles away, it does not matter. Love does not know distance. Real and true love is enduring and absolute.